"Read this book. It will ma ... if you will absorb and embody what Mike says. He addresses virtually every key issue in the journey of spiritual and emotional development. With personal and biblical examples (both joyous and difficult), Mike shows what it means to love the Lord with all one's heart, soul, mind, and strength. You will find practical steps to processing the hard things of life. You will find references to Brené Brown, Murray Bowen, Martha Nussbaum, St. John of the Cross, John Calvin, Martin Luther, Henri Nouwen, John O'Donohue, Augustine, C. S. Lewis, and Henry David Thoreau, to name a few. But it is not an academic exercise. This is a book born out of the pain of the 'in-between' spaces of life—the spaces of waiting, of having to let go of the past without yet knowing the realities of the future, of growing in one's capacity to entrust that to God. So read it. Pray it. Experience it."

—Jim Cofield,
co-author of *The Relational Soul*,
assistant director of CrossPoint Ministry

"Transition is often frightening, even paralyzing, but it can be a powerful opportunity for growth. Pastor Mike Brown takes us on a courageous spiritual journey in *Liminal: Transitions, Thresholds, and Waiting with God in the Space Between,* a soul-searching dive into growth and life. Written through his own experience and years of study, it serves as an introspective manual for learning how to wait on God. A brilliant contribution for growth and life in Christ."

—Jeff Ludington,
lead pastor of Generations Church

"There's something terrifying and magical about a 'stop.' These pauses in normal life are sometimes chosen by us, sometimes thrust upon us. I know I'm not the only one who would prefer they never occur, but they do. Mike offers all waiting souls a vision. In his words, 'There are some things that a productive life just doesn't prepare you for.' To that end, he clearly sets out the buffet of what God only chooses to do when we are stopped—and it's crucial. This book doesn't come from theory, but practice. It's credible and tangible. But, most importantly, it has helped me follow Jesus into the depths of who I really am—which is so much more valuable than what I attempt to do."

—Joseph Barkley,
pastor of Radius Church, Los Angeles

"In *Liminal: Transitions, Thresholds, and Waiting with God in the Space Between,* Mike Brown brings together profound biblical insight, ancient wisdom, and the wisdom that can only be gained through experience to help illuminate what are often the cloudy, in-between spaces of our lives—the liminal spaces between the old and the new, between death and resurrection. By vulnerably sharing his own story, as well as offering concrete spiritual practices for the journey, Mike serves as a guide to all of us who find ourselves in the place of waiting. This book is a gift, and I'm certain that the wisdom contained here will be beneficial to you as you walk the path of life."

—Drew Jackson,
author of *God Speaks through Wombs: Poems on God's Unexpected Coming,* pastor of Hope East Village, president of Pax

"Richard Rohr famously wrote about the 'spirituality of imperfection,' and in *Liminal: Transitions, Thresholds, and Waiting with God in the Space Between*, Mike Brown vulnerably shows us his loved version of it. Through his own personal journey of pain, the walk, and the refinement, he invites us into the liminal space where God does His best work in our souls. If this last couple of years has you questioning, Mike is a trusted guide through the pain and confusion because he has been there and walked through it himself. This book is a fantastic guide for the deeper work of soul transformation."

—**Steve Cuss,**
author of *Managing Leadership Anxiety,*
host of the *Managing Anxiety* podcast,
founder of the Capable Life online community

"If you're traversing between chapters of life, *Liminal: Transitions, Thresholds, and Waiting with God in the Space Between* is a timely work that offers insight for navigating through undefined transitions. This honest, transparent book provides intelligent thought drawn from rich resources and perspectives with depth for the in-between phases that are by nature nebulous. Whether you are looking for emotional health, better discipline, discipleship in all seasons, or—my favorite—unexpected creativity, Mike Brown, with these measures and more, shows you a way to embrace the in-between and grow from it."

—**Brian S. Chan,**
author of *The Purple Curtain*; lead pastor of Emmanuel Church,
Burbank; professor at Biola University

"Friends are safe places where you become more spacious. Mike Brown has been that kind of friend to me and my husband in the wilderness land of our own waiting. I'm overjoyed you will get to experience his presence through this book, welcoming you into the spacious place that is your invaluable soul."

—K. J. Ramsey,
licensed professional counselor,
author of *This Too Shall Last: Finding Grace When Suffering Lingers*

LIMINAL

TRANSITIONS, THRESHOLDS, AND WAITING WITH GOD IN THE SPACE BETWEEN

MIKE BROWN

LUCIDBOOKS

Liminal
Transitions, Thresholds, and Waiting with God in the Space Between

ISBN 978-1-63296-480-9 (paperback)
ISBN 978-1-63296-479-3 (ebook)

This book is dedicated to the Five:

Gracie, the fierce and fun-loving girl who taught me tenderness and gentleness.

Hudson, for your adventurous spirit and unconventional thinking.

Luke, the challenger, for your quiet strength and witty tongue.

Michael, for the conscientious drive that makes you the best of us.

But most of all for Amy, the green-eyed girl I grew up with and for.

TABLE OF CONTENTS

Φ
INTRODUCTION

You know the time, that the hour has come for you to wake from sleep. For salvation is nearer to us now than when we first believed. The night is far gone; the day is at hand.

—Rom. 13:11–12

You are in this time of the interim,
Where everything seems withheld.

The path you took to get here has washed out;
The way forward is still concealed from you.

"The old is not old enough to have died away;
The new is still too young to be born."

—John O'Donohue, "For the Interim Time"

When I was a child, I passed the time writing, drawing, reading books, riding my bike, and anything I could find to do until the next big thing. Of course, time passes differently in childhood. Christmas Eve lasts two weeks, waiting for the bell to ring on the last day of school takes a month, and lazy Sunday afternoons without television or video games is a year. Time seems to speed up with each passing year, and now I find myself complaining that the internet takes forever (several seconds), that I hit every traffic light on a short drive to the store (five minutes), and I have to wait forever (several weeks) for my tax refund to tell me what kind of vacation we'll be able to take that year. I belong to the generation that grew up analog yet now inhabits a digital adulthood. While I used to wait in front of the television for a song to come on so I could shush everyone and record it with my boom box, it now feels archaic to listen to a whole album of my favorite artist just to get to track nine. The thrill of hearing the electronic beeps and static while dialing up the internet was replaced forever with the instant nature of my first smartphone. The boredom that produced creativity, the waiting in silence, and the anticipation that gave birth to joy now seem more elusive and difficult. Of course, I am a culprit of my own making. Having traded my birthright for a steaming cup of instant coffee, I am guilty of getting exactly what I want when I want it.

The nature of the technological revolution combined with my own sinful impatience has mixed a disheartening cocktail. The very things my soul needs to flourish are the same things I now fight against with every fiber of my productive, effective being. Yet just as the rain falls on the just and unjust alike, so time washes over all of us. We are all given the same 24 hours in each day, seven days in a week, and 365 days in a year. The only thing in our control is how we pass the time, develop our character, and build our lives.

So what happens when how we spend our days is taken from us? Despite our hard work, we still find ourselves waiting for our big break. Our talent and gifts have not led to the future we imagined for ourselves. Through circumstances beyond our control, our boss overlooked us again for a promotion or recognition. Instead of being able to get to the next big thing in our lives, we are forced to wait and sit with the uncomfortable feeling of being neither here nor there, not who we once were but not yet being who we one day hope to be.

The passage from Romans 13 at the beginning of this Introduction speaks of the sunrise, that time of day neither fully lit by the sun nor fully clothed in darkness. It is an in-between time, and if you didn't know the time of day, you could easily confuse sunrise with sunset. It is precisely this season of our lives—the in-between—that this book is about.

By the grace of God, I can't deal with the subject of waiting as an expert, but I can show you what it is like as a traveler. Just when I feel I have mastered one type of waiting, another kind comes my way that feels fresh, painful, and new. Like it or not, these in-between periods of waiting are part of life. While most of us wouldn't choose waiting, we are never in control of the circumstances that lead to it, only how we respond. We can kick, scream, and cry "unfair," or we can learn how to follow Jesus into the valleys and forests as well as the mountaintops. And the experience of the mountaintop isn't possible without the experience of climbing it and toiling patiently day by day, no matter how mundane and routine the work seems. Who we are in the space between major events in our lives is what our life is built on.

You may find yourself at this moment in a period of incredible growth, creativity, and success. Or you may find yourself at a standstill, at war with who you truly are and who you want to be. You may find yourself in a boring season where everything is moving slowly, and one day leads to the next with little variation. You may be grieving the loss of a loved one, a job, a relationship, or a season of life you once enjoyed. You may also be just steps from arriving at your desired goal, seeing the light at the end of the tunnel while still aware of the darkness around you. This book was written during the COVID-19 pandemic of 2020, an event that made the year feel like all of the above. It was a hard reset of our lives, jobs, and schedules. We had to push pause on so much that brought us joy, provided meaning, and provided some kind of affirmation. A productive day for me in 2019 usually meant several meetings, working on a sermon, and leading a team at night. In 2020, I was proud that I had put my pants on to go to the store.

Regardless of where you are at this moment, this book is for you. While you most likely have already had lengthy periods of waiting, there are always more ahead. As Ralph Waldo Emerson once wrote, "Sow a thought and you reap an action; sow an act and you reap a habit; sow a habit and you reap a character; sow a character and you reap a destiny."[1] The seemingly linear path from thought to destiny turns out to be full of zigs and zags, lulls and peaks, heights and depths, excitement and boredom. As my wife and I frequently tell our children, you are not responsible for what your siblings did to you; you are only responsible for

---

1. "Ralph Waldo Emerson Quotes," Goodreads, accessed June 21, 2021, https://www.goodreads.com/quotes/416934-sow-a-thought-and-you-reap -an-action-sow-an.

how you choose to respond. We're not responsible for the landscape and terrain but only how we choose to respond to whatever comes our way.

I don't know if this happened only to kids who graduated in the 1990s, but my wife and I were both given a copy of Dr. Seuss's *Oh, the Places You'll Go!* for high school graduation. I remember it as an uplifting book about how we're going to crush the future, do nothing but win, and generally turn out better than anyone ever dreamed. My wife, who is a teacher and reads this to her students, encouraged me to read it again. That's how I found this passage:

> You can get so confused
> that you'll start in to race
> down long wiggled roads at a break-necking pace
> and grind on for miles across weirdish wild space
> headed, I fear, towards a most useless place.

He continues after several pages:

> I'm afraid that some times
> you'll play lonely games too.
> Games you can't win
> 'cause you'll play against you.
>
> All Alone!
> Whether you like it or not,
> Alone will be something
> you'll be quite a lot.
>
> And when you're alone, there's a very good chance
> you'll meet things that scare you right out of your pants.

There are some, down the road between hither and yon,
that can scare you so much you won't want to go on.

He continues after several pages:

Waiting for a train to go or a bus to come
or a plane to go or the mail to come
or the rain to go or the phone to ring,
or the snow to snow or waiting around for a Yes or No
or waiting for their hair to grow.

Everyone is just waiting.[2]

This is not bad advice, and the "waiting place" is understandably negative since waiting seems like a distraction to the main business of living life, moving from pinnacle to peak day by day. Instead, waiting often forces you to play "games you can't win 'cause you'll play against you." And therein lies the fruit. Waiting forces us to spend time alone in the palace of our minds, often discovering things about ourselves that can scare us so much we won't want to go on, things that can be discovered only in that still, silent place of inactivity. I've written this book with the hope that it will encourage others, give them perspective, and validate the common biblical advice to wait on God.

---

2. Dr. Seuss, *Oh, the Places You'll Go!* (New York: Random House, 1990), 23, 35.

Φ

CHAPTER ONE:
LIMINALITY

*It [liminality] is when you have left the tried and true,
but have not yet been able to replace it with anything
else. It is when you are between your old comfort zone
and any possible new answer. If you are not trained in
how to hold anxiety, how to live with ambiguity, how
to entrust and wait, you will run . . . anything to flee
this terrible cloud of unknowing.*

—Richard Rohr

Liminal comes from the Latin word *limens,* which means "threshold," a point of entry or beginning and therefore also a point of ending. It was first introduced to the field of anthropology to describe coming-of-age rituals that follow this three-part structure: separation, liminality (in between), and reassimilation. It can also be used to describe the grieving process when someone feels the loss of something (separation), enters into a transition period (liminality), and then ultimately reassimilates to a new normal.

It is the in-between space of past loss and future possibility where we need the most help. Victor Turner, the person responsible for exploring this concept further, calls liminal spaces "neither here nor there; they are betwixt and between the positions assigned and arrayed by law, custom, convention, and ceremony."[3] But Turner gives hope by referring to "betwixt and between" through the concept of the realm of pure possibility. What feels like pure loss of a way of living, a way of thinking, or a way of being in the world is actually an invitation to reimagine our lives and the joyful possibilities of living, feeling, and being different.

Examples of Liminal Spaces

To illustrate this concept, think about physical spaces as liminal. Stairwells and elevators are literally liminal spaces—neither here nor there, which is why an abandoned stairwell can feel creepy or "off." Hotel hallways may feel liminal late at night if you are walking through them alone since they are unfamiliar and strange and no one else is there. Schools during breaks, empty parking lots, and abandoned buildings are other examples of physical liminality.

Liminal mental states include major life transitions such as marriage, divorce, moving to a new place, or losing a job. We are familiar with the past and may have hopes for the future, but we are confronted with the off-putting *now*, which is where we are forced to live in the tension of what once was and what will be. The extent to which we have learned to be present in any given moment

---

3. Victor Turner, *The Ritual Process: Structure and Anti-Structure* (London: Cornell University Press, 1969); Victor W. Turner, "Passages, Margins, and Poverty: Religious Symbols and Communitas," in Victor W. Turner, *Dramas, Fields, and Metaphors: Symbolic Action in Human Society* (Ithaca, NY: Cornell University Press, 1974), 231.

largely dictates how we respond to periods of liminality in our lives. While writing this book, I was surrounded by moving boxes and was in a very real physical and mental space of liminality. The house we were moving out of represented memories, both good and bad; experiences with family, friends, and even strangers; and blood (quite literally since I am not a handyman), sweat, and tears from renovation. In spite of that history, at the end of our time there we could not inhabit the space the same way we had in the past. It became a kind of vehicle, a necessary waiting room to pass from one place to something more permanent.

Our new home, on the other hand, is nothing more than possibility and potential—potential memories, both good and bad; possible experiences with family, friends, and strangers; and a certainty of more blood, sweat, and tears of future renovation projects. It's betwixt and between, indeed, inhabiting only the realm of possibility.

Who are we in the middle? How do we live in a temporary season of life? Do we go on with business as usual, pretending it's not that bad in order to explain away the pain? Do we crumble under the weight of real loss and necessary change?

Liminal Spaces Require Change

Cross-cultural missionaries who return home have a lot to teach us about the experience of being a people in between two cultures—and neither is fully home. When they leave their home country, they willingly surrender their own cultural preferences for the sake of the gospel. They commit to learning a new language, culture, and worldview at the expense of the one they are most familiar with. There is a necessary end to the way they have lived in the world for the sake of something far greater than themselves. In this instance, it is the gospel mandate to go out of obedience to all nations, counting all as loss for the surpassing worth of knowing Jesus Christ, the Lord.[4] The in-between space is made more bearable if the weight of a God-given mission is behind it, right?

After living deeply among another people, missionaries tend to adopt some of the idiosyncrasies, mannerisms, taste for food, and forms of entertainment as the people they live among and love. Despite these similarities, they will never be one of the people groups they went to reach with the good news of Jesus. The native language, skin color, and first culture will always remind these missionaries of their "otherness." When they return home, though, they often find that, like themselves, the place they remember as familiar is also not the same.

Speaking of the need to grow and change by embracing necessary endings, Henry Cloud writes this:

> Whether we like it or not, endings are a part of life. They are woven into the fabric of life itself, both when it goes well, and also when it doesn't. On the good side of life, for us to ever get to a new level, a new tomorrow, or the next step, something has to end. Life has seasons, stages, and phases. For there to be anything new, old things always have to end, and we have to let go of them.[5]

For my wife, Amy, and me, this came as the loss of a career that had defined our marriage, our parenting, where we lived, and how we lived there. Yet the job simply represented the environment

---

4. See Phil. 3:7–8.
5. Henry Cloud, *Necessary Endings* (New York: HarperCollins Publishers, 2010), 6.

we allowed to shape us. Who we were in that environment both contributed to and was responsible for what and how we needed to change when it came time to leave that job. We lived the early years of our marriage with a painful lack of differentiation as seen through a flawed understanding of where we end and another begins. That led us to take responsibility for things outside of our control and personally receive criticism where none needed to be taken. Another area of unhealthiness was overfunctioning, or doing for others what they needed to do for themselves in order to grow. As a church planter and pastor, my church attracted many people whose tendency to underfunction caused us to do more and more under the guise of not wanting to create a burden for anyone else. More accurately, however, we didn't want to deal with the emotional consequences that would stem from stopping.

Another in-between space we can consider liminal is choosing to change how we've previously interacted at work, with friends, and in our homes. For my wife, that means she needs to acknowledge her need to be listened to, loved, and cared for. She must take the necessary time for herself and let go of obsessively caring for everyone around her. For me, that looks like recognizing latent insecurities and false narratives about the person I actually am rather than the person I would like to believe me to be. As always, busyness is not only the reality of this stage of life but also an easy escape from having to do the hard internal work of recognizing where unhealthy behaviors stem from, where relational patterns developed early in life, and ways we have been conditioned to respond to external stimuli.

This compulsive activity can be a way our souls hide from the things we need the most in order to avoid the pain of having to say no to things that distract us from doing the work, even the good things we enjoy. By staying busy at work (something I excel at), I can pretend I am actually doing better than I really am as I use external reality to justify my internal struggles. In the earliest days of beginning to wrestle with this, I lacked the vocabulary to even recognize what was going on inside, much less name it in order to confront it.

Those who are not used to recognizing their emotions typically have the hardest time with any process of exploring who they might be or become. We have mental crutches (drugs, entertainment, sex) we use to avoid the pain of self-exploration, or we may overidentify with the things we excel at (work, sports, school, intellectual pursuits), often throwing ourselves into activity as a means of numbing. We become emotional orphans, distant from others and unable to exercise true empathy or compassion, much less being able to describe how people, events, and circumstances make us feel. This attitude perfectly describes the early years of my marriage when my wife confronted me about her feelings about something. I deflected by trying to fix the problem or circumstance that led to her feeling that way. That type of behavior not only distances us from the people we love but also from the person we actually are, and it stunts our growth from becoming the people God is making us to be.

What I am fascinated with right now is the idea that liminality proves to be the necessary breeding ground for creativity (more on that in Chapter 5). Though most of us don't seek out these spaces, they are part of everyone's life. If we are not used to creating liminal spaces, we won't be able to capitalize on the opportunities they present or the invitation Jesus extends to follow Him in the in-between.

By creativity, I mean more than just art. I am referring to the invitation to imagine new ways of being us in the world, new patterns that lead to health and growth by shedding the well-worn skin of who we used to be. That process necessitates pain, the very thing we have been insulating ourselves from. In one of my favorite passages from *The Voyage of the Dawn Treader* by C. S. Lewis, the reader is introduced to Eustace Scrubb, a boy as critical and unpleasant as his name suggests. After stealing a magical bracelet that turns him into a dragon, he meets Aslan, who tells him to undress and enter a pool of water. Being a dragon, Eustace assumes that Aslan means for him to peel off his scales, which he does. Like an onion, though, he discovers there are multiple layers of scales that need to be peeled off, each one hurting more than the last. Finally, Aslan tells Eustace that he will need to undress him.

Lewis describes it in detail:

> *The very first tear was so deep that I thought it had gone right into my heart. And when he began pulling the skin off, it hurt worse than anything I've ever felt. . . . Well, he peeled the beastly stuff right off—just as I thought I had done it myself the other three times, only they hadn't hurt. . . . Then he caught hold of me—I didn't like that much for I was very tender underneath now that I'd no skin on—and threw me into the water. It smarted like anything but only for a moment. After that it became perfectly delicious and as soon as I started swimming and splashing I found that all the pain had gone from my arm. And then I saw why. I'd turned into a boy again.*[6]

---

6. C. S. Lewis, *The Voyage of the Dawn Treader* (New York: HarperCollins, 1952), 115–116.

When Eustace tried to undress himself, he was able to take superfluous layers off without it hurting, but as soon as he let Aslan do it, he felt immediate pain. I know this experience all too well—dying to the wrong things, making surface behavioral changes, and "sacrificing" things that might cost me physically but not emotionally. Second Corinthians 5:17 describes this process: "Therefore, if anyone is in Christ, he is a new creation. The old has passed away; behold, the new has come." What that passage does not describe is the liminal space between the old self dying and the new creation Jesus is making us to be. That is best explained by Jesus Himself when He told His disciples that if they desire to follow Him, "let him deny himself and take up his cross daily and follow me. For whoever would save his life will lose it, but whoever loses his life for my sake will save it. For what does it profit a man if he gains the whole world and loses or forfeits himself?" (Luke 9:23–25).

If it's true that this in-between space is a realm of pure possibility and the old has truly passed away, there is no limit to what the new creation might look like. It just requires the time and space to imagine. That typically means spending more time resting, playing, and doing nothing because down time is required to be able to creatively imagine a not-yet-realized future. The way we use our time and our difficulty to justify play and rest as necessary and valuable is also related to the concept of Sabbath, God's mandated means of helping us clarify who He is and who we are when we're not being defined by our work. When Moses introduced the concept of the Sabbath to the nation of Israel, he reminded them, "You shall remember that you were a slave in the land of Egypt, and the LORD your God redeemed you; therefore I command you this today" (Deut. 15:15).

Like the Jewish slaves in Egypt, we can remain imprisoned in our cell of activity, driven by harsh taskmasters telling us to push through, never quit, do more, and have unreasonable expectations of working without rest. Though our culture prizes busyness, this passage tells us that *if* we can't stop working, *if* we can't spend time in silence and solitude, and *if* we can't stand being alone with ourselves, we are every bit the slaves that God's people were before He redeemed them. Far from being a positive trait, busyness is an indictment that we don't actually know or trust the God of our salvation. How often have I substituted the life-giving relationship of being with Jesus for a life drained by working *for* Jesus? When we deny ourselves the God-given means of growth and life, we effectively become the god of our own lives—and fail miserably.

I recently read a story about Frank O'Brien, founder of Conversations, a fast-growing marketing service company. In response to the frantic pace of his industry, he initiated Do-Not-Call Monday.[7] It takes place on the first Monday of the month, normally a time for peak productivity. But instead of doing traditional work, he gathers all employees into a room for a full day. There are no phones allowed, no email, and no agenda. The entire day is spent getting away to think and talk. O'Brien understands that we need space to escape in order to discern what is essential and necessary, and in our time-starved culture, that doesn't happen by default—only by design. Put in context, O'Brien's planned liminality leads to greater clarity, productivity, and effectiveness.

To paraphrase Hebrews 11:15–16, if we continue thinking about where we came from, we will continually have the opportunity to stay there. But we desire a better place, that is, a heavenly one. Therefore, God is not ashamed to be called our God, for He has already prepared that place for us. Living in the realm of pure possibility requires us to make a decision. Despite the pain and cost associated with living in between the past and the future, how badly do we want things to change? Remember, it's rarely change itself that we fear; it's loss. Change represents the loss of something, someone, or someplace we have become accustomed to, whether it is healthy or not. What are we willing to say no to in order to create the space to think with clarity about a preferred future? Here are some worthwhile questions so you can explore this personally.

1. What is causing you the greatest amount of anxiety right now? What do you fear most? The answers to these questions will help you shed light on your obstacles to growth. If we are not aware of our fears and anxieties, they are certainly controlling us more than we realize.

2. What are you most afraid of being true about yourself? What is the false narrative you believe about the person you would like to believe you are? These questions take the process one step further, allowing us to do business with the shame and guilt that drive us to act as we do. Shame and guilt are both powerful motivators and fuel us to run ourselves into the ground and keep up a pretense for ourselves and others. Without an honest assessment of our weaknesses, our living sacrifices become nothing but empty husks, shadows of who we are and what we need Jesus to redeem.

3. What do you need to say no to in order to create the space needed to think deeply about your preferred future? We are kidding ourselves if we think we can maintain the

frantic pace of our lives while fitting this kind of soul searching into an already maxed-out schedule. If we are not willing to say no to something we enjoy or feel we need, that is a sure sign that an area of our life is controlling us more than we realize. Why do we feel we need all our activities? What is the trade-off we make in order to include them? In the 1970s, Southwest Airlines began a daunting strategy of saying no to things other airlines took for granted. The strategy included flying to limited major destinations, not serving meals, letting people choose seats instead of assigning them, and offering no first-class section. It seemed like business suicide. But when their strategy began to pay off, Continental Airlines tried to straddle that strategy by keeping their existing systems intact while also adopting their competitor's strategy. They began to offer Continental Lite, mimicking some of Southwest's practices. But trying to adopt one strategy without sacrificing another cost them hundreds of millions of dollars in the end. Ignoring the reality of trade-offs is a terrible strategy for both businesses and people.

4. What makes you the most excited about living differently than you are now? What is the joy set before us that would lead to enduring the cross, despising the shame?[8] What is the potential for our relationships flourishing with Jesus, our spouse, our children, and our friends? What is the benefit to enduring the liminal to press through to the eternal? How might we actually be better people by engaging in this process?

---

8. See Heb. 12:2.

One thing is clear—our participation by taking intentional action has been, is, and will be a reality for every one of us. Whether by design or by circumstance, the living God is at work bringing these choices to us, inviting us into something deeper and truer. There is no escape from the liminal; it's just a choice to either do the hard work, delay it by numbing ourselves and pretend things are not that bad, or simply ignore God and run away. A friend once told me that the process of change is always harder and takes much longer than we thought. My friend then gave me more bad news and told me this process typically takes three to five years before we bear real fruit.[9] For a culture built on instant gratification, that seems like a bad trade-off. For followers of Jesus, the time discipleship actually takes seems like a reasonable offer.

So we step into the difficult without expectation of immediate release, taking one step forward and several back. Like toddlers, we have to learn to walk and talk, this time much differently than we used to. We sacrifice the illusion of being in control and instead cling to Jesus's promise to make all things new.[10] We move from begrudgingly admitting our physical, intellectual, and relational limits to glorying in the grace His divinity brings to our humanity. And in so doing, we become real men and women of substance, not simply shadows of who we might have been.

---

9. The Transtheoretical Model talks about this (Prochaska & DiClemente, 1983; Prochaska, DiClemente & Norcross, 1992; Prochaska & Velicer, 1997). The study, which focused on establishing healthy behaviors, found that after 12 months of health habits, 43 percent failed to maintain their healthy habit. It was not until five years of maintenance that the risk for relapse dropped to 7 percent.
10. See Rev. 21:5.

Waiting on God

The Bible is full of authors who describe in detail the liminal spaces they encountered in their lives. Consider the amount of waiting every man and woman of God who are our examples had to experience. Sarah, Rebekah, and Hannah all suffered from infertility and waited their whole adult lives for children. Abraham waited 25 years between God promising him a son and Isaac being born. Moses was 80 years old before God used him to deliver the Israelites, and he would spend another 40 years wandering in the wilderness with them. The Apostle Paul was a Christian 10 years before his first missionary journey when he actually began the work of being the apostle to the Gentiles. King David was on the run from Saul for more than 13 years. It took the Apostle John a lifetime of following Jesus to change from being a Son of Thunder to the Apostle of Love.[11]

Whether or not we endure seasons of waiting on God is not up to us. Yet there is ample biblical precedent for how we should think, act, and live while we wait. Our sound-bite, instant-gratification culture does not prepare us to live in service to the Lord over the years. We have been promised to have our lives changed by signing up for a 16-week class or saying a prayer that asks God to enlarge our territory.[12] We expect immediate change when coming to Jesus because, after all, the old has gone and the new has come, right? (More on that in Chapter 6).

Lamentations was written after one of the darkest moments in Israel's history. The author, Jeremiah the prophet, wrote this:

The LORD is good to those who wait for him,
*   to the soul who seeks him.*

---

11. See Mark 3:17, 1 John 4:7–21.
12. See 1 Chron. 4:10.

It is good that one should wait quietly
 for the salvation of the LORD.
It is good for a man that he bear
 the yoke in his youth.

—Lam. 3:25–27

That's a hard thing to say while sitting on the rubble of Jerusalem that had just been destroyed by the Babylonian army. There was no resolution, no end in sight. In fact, the bulk of Lamentations is full of just that—a lament over a city razed, people violated, and justice perverted. How is it good for a person to bear the yoke of waiting quietly for the Lord when it seems like nothing is happening? Perhaps the greatest perspective shift comes when we can identify what we're waiting for.

Merriam-Webster defines *wait* as "to remain stationary in readiness or expectation." Remaining stationary when God is not answering your requests is a difficult thing. What if we weren't waiting with expectation for God to do anything? What would it look like to remain ready to encounter new depths of God's love and concern for us, regardless of circumstances? The content of our waiting is just as important as our posture during it. The very fact that we are forced to wait puts our impatience on display. When we are not in control of the outcomes, the circumstances, and other people, we begin to get antsy.

One of the first signs in my life that I'm not doing okay is an incessant desire to subdue my surroundings. It doesn't matter what is currently surrounding me as long as I can exert my will upon it in a tangible way. In a matter of hours, I walk around the house and handle four projects I've been procrastinating. I "beat my body and bring it into submission" (1 Cor. 9:27 WEB) and push it to the limit. I clean the kitchen grout with a toothbrush until it sparkles. It really doesn't matter what I'm subduing as long as I feel in control.

Waiting on God removes our feeling of control and forces us to look elsewhere in order to subdue that emotion. My hands are truly bound, I am incapable of changing my circumstances, and no amount of whining or fighting will change that. As Henry Cloud says, "What I want to do here is to get specific about what those elements of character are that make it all go one way or the other, and in doing so, to give you a helpful template by which to grow into the person who can deliver whatever reality asks you to do. . . . Reality is always your friend."[13] Waiting takes my lip service of trusting in God and forces me to confront the reality of what that space between looks like in practice. Lamentations encourages us to sit alone and keep silent because God has laid it on us. Silence implies an acceptance of God's timing and a refusal to complain to others.

If God is the author of this season and is asking me to wait in silence, then I must trust (have faith), and there is a good reason for it. That reason may have nothing to do with my happiness or fulfillment in the present moment, a concept that requires an expansion of our vocabulary of experiences with the Lord God Almighty. Just because I can't draw a direct line from an experience to my happiness does not mean the experience is not necessary, good, and right. It just means that some extra work is required on my part to lean into the awkward and the uncomfortable. It makes sense.

While many of us would not subscribe to a health-and-wealth theology, we functionally believe and live like we do. So much of our understanding of God's desires for us centers on our prosper-

---

13. Henry Cloud, *Integrity: The Courage to Meet the Demands of Reality* (New York: HarperCollins Publishers, 2009), Google Books, 26, 106.

ity, blessing, and success. We speak of God's blessing synonymous with our finances. We tell others how good God has been because of the health we've enjoyed recently. And a promotion at work could only be God's favor, despite the fact that this blessing will take us away from our family and our church community, leaving us with less time for the things we say matter most to us. There is always a gap between what we say we believe to be true and how we functionally appropriate that. This is not necessarily a negative thing as long as we are paying attention to what the gap is between our understanding of God and our experience with Him.

Waiting on God also helps us develop a greater trust in His sovereignty throughout history. The ability to tolerate delayed gratification has never been the human race's strongest suit. Just because we don't see anything happening (on the surface at least) doesn't mean God is not actively at work in and through the fabric of time and space. Much of our collective history consists of long years of fallowness when nothing seemed to be happening, at least nothing observable. The common thread of how God works in our lives and how God works in history is that *God works*. Seen and unseen, miraculous and mundane, across continents and in unknown villages, God is always working out His perfect plan in His often inscrutable ways. As we wait for weeks, months, or possibly years for Him to bring some answers to our questions or relief to our struggles, we learn to look for His light, wherever it may be found.

Sometimes when it becomes difficult to find God in the evident and obvious, we become better at seeing His work in the rote and routine. A visit from a friend we feel safe with reminds us how God works through community. A particularly good bottle of wine reminds us we were created to savor and enjoy. An unexpected comment or turn of phrase becomes the voice of Jesus assuring us. If we were never forced to wait on the Lord, we would never develop the sensitivity and patience to wait and watch for Him in the small as well as the large. As Moses told the Israelites before God parted the Red Sea, "The LORD will fight for you, and you have only to be silent" (Exod. 14:14).

Another fruit of waiting is that it helps us clarify where our hope truly lies. The prophet Micah said, "But as for me, I will look to the LORD; I will wait for the God of my salvation; my God will hear me" (Mic. 7:7). It's easy for me to think I believe in the goodness of God when my bank account and belly are full. The real test is when that belief goes against all evidence and we still choose to persevere and recommit our trust daily in the living God. As we sit with bitterness, anger, and disappointment with God and our lives, the source of our frustrations typically become clearer. We had unmet expectations, unpromised desires, and unexpected suffering, and no one prepared us for a life of discipleship in the frustrating middle. We came to Jesus with a rush of excitement for our new life in Christ, our forgiveness of sin, and our empowerment by His Spirit with grace available to us each new day.

Predictably, not many of us were told that "all who desire to live a godly life in Christ Jesus will be persecuted" (2 Tim. 3:12) and that the world will hate you (see John 15:18). Some turn away at this point, feeling duped and taken advantage of. These are the people you may hear say, "I tried Jesus when I was younger, but it didn't work for me." It's interesting that we develop expectations of what following Jesus will entail independent of the Bible, filling in gaps in our understanding with culturally accepted norms and clichés. We are largely unaware of these expectations until they are not met, and when Jesus doesn't do what He never promised to do, we blame Him. What a unique gift waiting is! When we move through the initial disappointment and start getting curious about what's going on under the surface of our emotions, we find an opportunity to truly put our hope in the person of Jesus.

Waiting often helps us notice the pace of our walk with God. John Piper notes, "Waiting on the Lord is the opposite of running ahead of the Lord, and it's the opposite of bailing out on the Lord. It's staying at your appointed place while he says *stay,* or it's going at his appointed pace while he says *go.*"[14] As a runner, I have to adjust my body to a natural pace so it can endure long-distance running. I can train my body to increase my pace, but I can never ignore it. If I am pushing too hard, there are potential injuries guaranteed to slow me down. If I am running too slowly, I will feel my body wanting to run a little faster. Often, periods of waiting come alongside periods of pain, hurt, and frustration. This is an invitation to slow down and pay attention to the places we ought to be giving our attention. There is a required slowness from our pain that forces us to confront our humanness and bring our whole self to God to heal and to bless. There may be seasons of sprinting in the future, but after enjoying a more responsive, contemplative pace, we might decide against a more hurried lifestyle.

As a leader in the church, I had mental categories for things that required my attention. There were the one-and-done decisions that didn't require too much focus or effort, such as deciding to hire an outside graphic designer or finding a volunteer in the church. Then there were the decisions best made as a staff in order to get more input, learn other ideas, and think through outcomes or potential pitfalls. Finally, there were the kind of landscape-altering changes that required extensive prayer, discussion,

---

14. John Piper, *Future Grace, Revised Edition: The Purifying Power of the Promises of God* (Colorado Springs, CO: Multnomah Books, 2012), 246.

waiting, and evaluation. They required all our attention over a period of time, all our emotional intelligence to uncover fears and anxieties that might emerge, and all our spiritual depth to know the heart, mind, and will of God in the situation. I've never regretted those times we chose to move slowly, think things through, and seek God's desires for our church. The mistakes I made happened when I moved too quickly in my zeal without accounting for how others would feel or respond to change and loss. Once a season of waiting forces us to slow down, it becomes easier and easier to modulate our pace as we move forward in the future. We will instinctively know when we have been moving too fast, taking on too much, and requiring some time for rest and reflection. It's yet another gift of learning to wait well.

Seasons of helplessness and hopelessness should form a deep humility in us—a deep, soul-level recognition of our earthliness and spiritual poverty. Truly we came from and will return to the dust of the earth. Yet during our time here on earth, we continually find ourselves boasting about our strength and victory before we've even dressed for battle.[15] It's hard not to boast in our wisdom when we are often told by others how our ideas and words have impacted them. It's hard not to boast in our strength when others often praise us for our resilience, our drive, and our never-say-die attitude. It's hard not to boast in our riches when our financial security provides for us and others so well, and we really don't need any help.[16] It's when all that is either taken away or stripped of its power that we are confronted with the poverty of our riches, the foolishness of our wisdom, and the weakness

---

15. See 1 Kings 20:11.
16. See Jer. 9:23.

of our strength.[17] We are offered a glimpse of life through the Father's eyes where He chooses to exalt the things that seem like nothing to show His power. It is then that any boasting is on behalf of God who has bought our lives with the high price through the blood of Jesus.

When I find myself becoming increasingly impatient and upset at my inability to change a season of waiting, I need to remind myself that God is the one who put me here. Even if I am responsible for poor life decisions that are negatively affecting me, God has not been caught off guard. He is not surprised or scrambling to execute plan B. The God of time, space, and human history has designed me to be in this very place at this very moment. And while I may buck against that place, it is a reminder that my life is truly not my own. I am a breath, a vapor, a quick flash of light and life in the scope of the universe. Yet I am known, desired, and accepted, and the Father will take care of me well.

Humility is when we see the immensity of God's power alongside His utter tenderness and compassion with our small, short lives. I am an adopted son who now belongs in the family of God through no merit of my own. My Father has stopped me from running full steam to pursue something that seems right to me, without knowing whether it will lead to life or death.[18] In that truth I can finally see myself as I truly am and God for who He truly is. He is not hemming me in to thwart me, nor is He obstructing the flow of goodness and joy arbitrarily. He is working for my good and His glory. I need to get over myself and realize that if I am being forced to wait, surely He is developing

---

17. See 1 Cor. 1:26–31.
18. See Prov. 14:12.

something better in me. God owes me nothing but has given me everything I need, often when I can't tell the difference.

The last paradox of waiting is that just when we feel we have nothing left, He not only gives power to the weak but actually increases our strength.[19] Isaiah the prophet says, "Even youths shall faint and be weary, and young men shall fall exhausted; but they who wait for the LORD shall renew their strength; they shall mount up with wings like eagles; they shall run and not be weary; they shall walk and not faint" (Isa. 40:30–31).

Just as Jesus came for those who are sick rather than the healthy, notice who the recipients of His strength are—the weak. Human weakness is the prerequisite to receiving divine strength. We simply don't think we need it when we feel self-sufficient. It is in our felt weakness when we are moved to acknowledge our limits and receive His help. How do we receive that strength? We get it by waiting. It's not passively accepting that God put the brakes on our plans but actively asking, seeking, and knocking on His door. It comes by developing a holy curiosity about our inner lives and asking the hard questions. It's not settling for His guidance without His presence.[20]

Isn't this process reminiscent of how we came to Jesus in the first place? We didn't come by standing tall but by kneeling in contrition. We could not merit our place in His family, and we freely admitted our weakness and frailty through repentance. In return, we were clothed with the righteousness of Christ,[21] justified through faith, and we exchanged our weakness for His strength. The narrow door by which we came to Jesus was and is marked by

19. See Isa. 40:29.
20. See Exod. 33:15.
21. See Isa. 61:10.

weakness, and we never graduate from that posture. The words *weak* (Isa. 40:29) and *faint* (Isa. 40:30) are from the same Hebrew word, which means "failure through loss of inherent strength." The word *weary* in Isaiah 40:30 comes from a different word that means "exhaustion because of the hardness of life."[22] Regardless of the source of our weariness and weakness, Jesus stands ready to give us His strength. Yet the last verse of Isaiah 40 modifies the use of that strength. Notice the progression from flying with eagles' wings to running and not being weary and then to walking and not growing faint. As I mentioned earlier about the pace of our life in Christ, this strength is not meant to support a lifetime of continual flight but rather an ordinary plodding through the unremarkable and mundane, finding Jesus at work in both.

Discipleship in the Space Between

Part of what is broken in the Western church is that we've made discipleship a process of learning the right things and adding in a couple of practices to reinforce them rather than studying one thing that will take us a lifetime to master. Some people say that authors typically write one book over and over again. That makes sense since the Spirit works in each of us uniquely, giving us a message, an approach, a passion, and a distinctive way of looking at the world around us. We are largely unaware of such personal distinctiveness until later in our lives. As we grow older and gain experience, we are able for the first time to look backward as well as forward, identifying commonalities that have been with us through the years. We see patterns emerge in the times of our lives

---

22. David Guzik, "Study Guide for Isaiah 40" in *The Enduring Word Commentary*, Blue Letter Bible, accessed June 21, 2021, https://www.blbclassic.org/commentaries/comm_view.cfm?AuthorID=2&contentID=23658&commInfo=217&topic=Isaiah.

we felt most alive and engaged. We can track both consolations and desolations—the things that drew us closer to God and the things that pushed us away. We more quickly see the kinds of situations that will likely make us feel anxious and the kinds of situations we excel in. This is a gift to our growth as students of Jesus since the flipside of knowing God more deeply is knowing ourselves.

Far from spiritual navel-gazing or self-love, the virtue of self-examination as a means of knowing God is ancient. Saint Augustine prayed, "O God, always the same, let me know myself, let me know you."[23] John Calvin wrote this in his book *Institutes of the Christian Religion*:

> *Nearly all the wisdom which we possess, that is to say, true and sound wisdom, consists of two parts: the knowledge of God and of ourselves. But, while joined by many bonds, which one precedes and brings forth the other is not easy to discern. . . . Without knowledge of self, there is no knowledge of God. Without knowledge of God, there is no knowledge of self.*[24]

This is discipleship. The initial growth phase of our walk with Jesus consists of learning a lot about Him. It makes sense that after living as long as we did apart from Jesus we need a lot of deconstruction and reconstruction. We hold attitudes, habits, assumptions, worldviews, and a thousand other things that we

---

23. "Living the Christian Life. Let Me Know Myself, Let Me Know You: This Is Prayer," Catholic Online, accessed June 21, 2021, https://www.catholic.org/news/hf/faith/story.php?id=47147.
24. John Calvin, *Institutes of the Christian Religion,* translated by Henry Beveridge (Peabody, MA: Hendrickson Publishers, 2008), 4.

must bring into the light of the gospel. And just as we lived apart from Jesus for so long, we also lived apart from our true selves. We leaned into lies and deception, afraid to face the truth about ourselves. Like Adam and Eve, we wrapped ourselves in fig leaves of our own making, hoping to hide from God, others, and self.

Henri Nouwen gives us this encouragement:

> *Find the courage to enter into the core of our own existence and become familiar with the complexities of our own inner lives. As soon as we feel at home in our own house, discover the dark corners as well as the light spots, the closed doors as well as the drafty rooms, our confusion will evaporate, our anxiety will diminish, and we will become capable of creative work.*[25]

Nouwen is speaking about articulating our own experiences of God's work in us so we can help others on their journey. This is not simply a cerebral aspect of discipleship where we continue to learn what was hidden from us before the Spirit of the living God took up residence in our souls. By definition, to *know* (*yada* in Hebrew, *gnosis* in Greek) someone or something in Scripture is to know it through personal experience. Adam's sexual intimacy with his wife is referred to as "knowing her." This is knowledge of self and God in the most tangible, experiential way possible.

It is when we are stuck in the space between, waiting on God, that we become acquainted with being this kind of an apprentice to Jesus. Waiting creates the environment where this kind of learning in the classroom of life can happen. It reminds me of the way Jesus

---

25. Henri Nouwen, *The Wounded Healer: Ministry in Contemporary Society* (New York: Doubleday, 1979), 38.

teaches His disciples in the Gospel of Luke. First, He introduces them to the concept of faith. They all respond positively, assuring Jesus they understand and have faith. Then He takes them into a boat and promptly falls asleep right before a storm hits. Now they have the opportunity to exercise that faith, but instead, they freak out and tell Jesus they're going to die. He rebukes the elements, and as the wind dies down and the waves grow calm, He asks the disciples about the faith they just said they understood so well.[26] This is how spiritual muscles become stronger. It's too easy to assume we understand something we've just learned before we've had a chance to practice it. It's one thing to listen to a sermon from someone who has lived what they are talking about; it's another to have God engineer your circumstances so you have to do so on your own.

Courage

This is not an easy thing to step into. In our natural state, we tend to shrink back from pain, brokenness, and difficulty. Some of us equate any difficulty in our lives with a lack of God's blessing, thus pronouncing divine failure over a project we haven't yet started. We miss out on the greater, deeper, truer good that comes from really hard and messy work because we can't see how God's hand could be in something so hard and seemingly hopeless.

At the same time, we know that the most often repeated statements in Scripture are some variation of either have courage or do not be afraid. We are told, "Do not be anxious about anything" (Phil. 4:6), "Do not be anxious about tomorrow, for tomorrow will be anxious for itself" (Matt. 6:34), "Be strong and courageous. Do not fear" (Deut. 31:6), and "Be watchful, stand

---

26. See Luke 8

firm in the faith, act like men, be strong" (1 Cor. 16:13). The Bible has literally dozens of similar commands. One of my favorite commands comes from the book of Joshua when Israel's new leader is listening to the Lord for direction after the death of Moses. Joshua is understandably nervous, standing in the immense shadow of his predecessor and more than a little fearful of any possible outcome. Moses led a group of forgetful slaves to freedom, collapsing the leadership structure of the greatest national superpower of the day. In order to do so, God performed some pretty top-shelf miracles to substantiate Moses's claims of authority and a God-given mandate. After parting an entire mini ocean so His people could cross on dry land, God allowed the Red Sea to collapse on their pursuers.

Throughout 40 years of trials and complaining, Moses was a prototypical adaptive leader, taking people who wanted to return to Egypt to a future reality instead. To lead a people that stubborn and stiff-necked, Moses had to be grounded in something. So they were big shoes for Joshua to fill, and on top of that, God just told him he is to lead the newly bereft people into the Promised Land, subdue the land and their enemies, and govern a people who had proved in the wilderness to be nearly ungovernable. Knowing the weight of this responsibility, God encourages Joshua at length:

> *Just as I was with Moses, so I will be with you. I will not leave you or forsake you. Be strong and courageous, for you shall cause this people to inherit the land that I swore to their fathers to give to them. Only be strong and very courageous, being careful to do according to all the law that Moses my servant commanded you. Do not turn from it to the right hand or to the left, that you may have good success wherever you go. This*

*Book of the Law shall not depart from your mouth,
but you shall meditate on it day and night, so that you
may be careful to do according to all that is written
in it. For then you will make your way prosperous,
and then you will have good success. Have I not
commanded you? Be strong and courageous. Do not
be frightened, and do not be dismayed, for the LORD
your God is with you wherever you go.*

—Josh. 1:5–9

Even reading that now, I get fired up. I feel like I could take on an army or scale a wall. I feel secure and cared for. With God behind, before, and in me, I believe there is nothing too difficult. And that's the point of God's encouragement to Joshua. He will be with him *wherever* he goes. It's easy to extrapolate this encouragement outward for the external task Joshua is about to undertake, but what about the equally necessary internal journey we must take before the outward comes to pass? Courage sounds great when it comes to picking up a sword and slaying some fools. But when I need to have the courage to pick up a mirror and look honestly at the fool who has made a mess of his own life, it seems difficult.

Make no mistake, the courage required to have hard conversations at work, to choose integrity over convenience, and to continually show up in difficult spaces to love difficult people is still courage when it comes to doing our own inner work and identifying our fears, our insecurities, and our demons. We need courage to be honest with ourselves, especially if we have surrounded ourselves with people who are also afraid to do that. Without an honest assessment of where we've been and where we are, we will never chart the future path to where we hope to be.

We need courage because all of us, without exception, spent our childhoods learning how to be us in the world. We observed people and events around us, made interpretations of those things, and told ourselves a story about how to remain safe in that world. Some of these stories are true, some of them are false, but we've interpreted most of them badly. This is the work of discipleship, friendship, community, marriage, therapy, and countless other means of grace and growth. I firmly believe that the best gift we can give to the world is a life rightly interpreted, making sense of our stories in light of God's story revealed in Scripture.

We need not fear liminal spaces when they serve as a reminder that we, too, are an already-but-not-yet Kingdom people. We are already justified by faith, adopted by the Father, and able to walk by faith in Jesus in His Kingdom now. We eagerly await the consummation of His Kingdom at the end of all things when we are revealed as the glorious sons and daughters of God.[27] We live in the twilight of this present world and the sunrise of the one to come. We can embrace both realities—who we are and who we will be when we finally see Jesus.

---

27. See Rom. 8:23, 1 John 3:2.

Φ

CHAPTER TWO: A PERSONAL JOURNEY TO THE SPACE BETWEEN

Some of you just sit there smoking
And some are already sold.
This is the age you are broken
Or turned into gold.
This is the age you are broken or turned into gold.
                                        —Antonia Michaelis

But to understand, someone has said, a man must
stand under.
                                        —Frederick Douglass

People may call what happens at midlife "a crisis," but it's
not. It's an unraveling—a time when you feel a desperate
pull to live the life you want to live, not the one you're
"supposed" to live. The unraveling is a time when you are
challenged by the universe to let go of who you think you
are supposed to be and to embrace who you are.
                                        —Brené Brown

The Middle-of-Life Reckoning

"How old are you?" my spiritual director asked. "I'm 38," I answered. "Well, you're a little early, but still right on time for your midlife reckoning." I had no idea yet how true or how often those words would come back to me over the next five years.

There is a reason the famed midlife crisis receives so much attention in popular culture. Sure, it's easy to poke fun at the 55-year-old who still wears skinny jeans, dyes his hair, and trades the minivan for a Mini Cooper as soon as the kids leave. Forty has become an almost mythical number to us, seemingly ancient to the young and so young to those on the other side of it. Whatever the reason, age does seem to delineate our lives into two halves. First used by Carl Jung, the idea of two halves helps determine the task of the first half, which is to build a sense of identity, structure, and security. And the second half deconstructs those in order to find a deeper source of meaning and purpose.

The first half of our lives is largely full of things to look forward to. That gives the process of waiting a boundary we can deal with, assuring ourselves that good things and greater joys are just around the corner. When I turned 16 and could get my driver's license, I knew that would be the answer to the stifling regime of living under my parents' roof. When I turned 18 and could legally buy a lottery ticket and cigarettes (which I had already been bumming off friends for two years), I had the simple joy of looking forward to winning the lottery or never going without a nicotine fix. When I turned 21, the lure of alcohol was already well established, but then I could get into clubs without using a fake ID or devising some type of manipulation to buy beer. It gave my life a whole new layer of fun. When I turned 22, I had a life-changing encounter with Jesus, and all that came before was garbage in light of all I had to relearn and look forward to with Him. That encounter was the moment that gave my life meaning, purpose, and excitement.

The day after I met Jesus, I met my future wife, which brought all the rush and excitement of a new relationship and the future possibilities it held. During our dating period, I had an unmistakable calling from Jesus to leave my successful sales career in order to pursue full-time ministry. There was such purity and naïveté to it that I thought it would simply be the means to love Jesus and love His people while being able to earn a living doing something I already loved. Intoxicated by a new life in Christ, new career, and new marriage, Amy and I had our first child several years after our wedding day, and that changed the landscape of our lives. Never again would it be just the two of us, but we didn't yet know the effect it would have on our lives. Like most new parents, we were tired but so hopeful for our firstborn and our future. The following years brought us two more sons, one daughter, and several foster children, each bringing their own period of hopefulness and joy.

I was an assistant pastor at a church when we again heard the unmistakable voice of Jesus calling us to move to Mexico where we had been taking short-term mission teams for a year or so. We had concerns about the way we saw Americans engaging cross-culturally and thought we could be part of the solution. Packing up our little family, we sold most of our things and moved to a village outside of Tecate, ready to experience a life of simplicity, goodness, and excitement in Christ. We had our whole future as missionaries to look forward to, and despite a rocky first year, we eventually acclimated to life in a small, rural village in another country. Then we found out we had to leave and again heard the unmistakable voice of Jesus (this time through good friends) encouraging us to plant a new church in Los Angeles. Devastated by the loss of the life we thought we were going to live but buoyed by the hope of a new adventure, we moved back to Los Angeles to experience church planting. There was an intoxicating mix of youthful optimism, high ideals, and rigid conviction about the kind of New Testament community we wanted to create right in the city we loved. This season of our lives provided more than its share of new experiences, great highs and lows, exciting challenges, and uncertain risks.

Yet time marches on, waiting for no one, and one day you look up from the grind and find yourself older than you remember. You find the age gap between the youth in your church and your own generation growing larger by the year. I was 10 years into church planting when I first experienced a forced liminal time, knowing I had to reevaluate the way I was living but not knowing what to do instead.

I was blissfully unaware of a shriveling inner life, a stunted emotional and relational capacity, and a myriad of coping mechanisms to have something to look forward to. The challenges of the first half of my life were mitigated by never having to wait long for God. I always had something to do, enough energy to do it, and rarely had a break to take a breath or take stock of why I was doing it in the first place. It was just a restless urgency—so prized in the business world—that allowed me to stay on the treadmill of productivity, not making huge progress but still sweating and looking busy in the process.

The amazing thing about this is that I understood, taught, and even said I cherished the dichotomy between being and doing. Our being precedes our doing, and our doing must come from our being. Who we are in Christ is more important than what we do for Him. These and other platitudes would roll from my lips so easily that I must have believed them. Yet apparently, the gap between believing and living is wider than the space between being and doing. In order to rightly emphasize my being, I needed a season where my idolatry of doing would be violently crushed, ground into powder, and forced down my throat.[28]

Somewhere along the way in life, I picked up certain skills to make life better, more enjoyable, and safer for me. I became driven, a hard worker, always giving 110 percent. I learned that walking with assumed confidence inspires real confidence and respect from others. I learned that if you never let anyone in too close, they can't hurt you. I learned that if you punch first and punch hard, you don't have to fight too often after that. None of this is particularly unique to me or uncommon. We all find ways to be us in the world, dictated by circumstances, personal tastes, proclivities, and desires. Some of those are positive expressions of the people we were created to be, called the true self by my favorite contemplative, Thomas Merton. Others are strategies of our false selves in order to cope with the pain and suffering life inevitably brings to every living thing under the sun.

Hitting the Wall

Shortly after this season of being unaware yet productive, I experienced what some call hitting the wall. That happens often in midlife when our strategies for coping have been working well until one day they don't. At that point, we are old enough to know better than to go back to some of the strategies of our youth but young enough to still try other ways to mask the attention our soul needs. Suddenly the unmistakable voice of Jesus becomes a little less clear. Our future steps, previously illuminated, go

---

28. See Exod. 32:20.

dark. The goodness right around the corner becomes a source of fear and anxiety at the unknown. For me, it led to doubling down on work, being productive and efficient, and grasping tightly to everything I had built that there was no room to rest lest it all be taken from me. I can feel the tension building in my shoulders now as I write this, remembering that season of my life. I became like Jacob before his limp—a deceiver, a grasper, an image builder. The weight of this life I had built was now on my shoulders to maintain, and since I had no understanding of my limitations, I felt pretty good about my ability to go the distance with it on my back.

In May 2015, I attended a conference where I heard a life-changing message about burnout, defined as "an inner restlessness with underlying anxiety that leads to compulsory ministry, accentuating functionality over spiritual communion with Christ."[29] That definition described me perfectly, and I sought out the speaker for spiritual direction. As I was slowly becoming vaguely aware of my emotions and the damage I was doing to my body through ceaseless activity, the remainder of that year brought more pain, loss, and grief than I had ever experienced. We had close friends leave Los Angeles—common for those in big cities, but the loss never gets easier—a church conflict, and betrayals that opened old wounds of abandonment I didn't know were still there. To top it off, as I was healing from an invasive surgery, I got news that my kid brother had had a heart attack at age 31 and had died. Shortly after his death, I was in my car driving to his apartment in central California to make a value judgment on his earthly possessions, deciding what to keep and

---

29. Rich Plass and Jim Cofield, Presentation at Acts 29 US West Conference, Reno, Nevada, May 5, 2015.

what to sell the very next day. There are some things a productive life just doesn't prepare you for. This was one of those things. The next few years felt like God was incrementally turning up the burner I was sitting on, forcing me to evaluate the present and ask different questions about what I wanted the future to look like.

Into the Liminal Unknown

After I took an honest look at my gifts, my desires, and my hopes for the second half of life, my wife and I decided to turn the church over to someone else and leave full-time pastoral ministry for the first time in almost 20 years. I had to lose the world I had created for myself to gain the integrity of my soul. Throughout my life and ministry, I have had a front-row seat to pastors shipwrecking their lives because of deep-seated unhealthy patterns, unaddressed trauma, and unmet expectations. There was one season in particular when several peers either disqualified themselves through sin or took their own lives. Others lived in chronic depression and despair because they felt the only job their biblical education qualified them for was pastoral ministry. How would they provide for their families if they left the ministry? I was asking myself a different question, though. How long would I have before my own inner turmoil caught up to me in the same way? There is a stigma associated with pastors who choose to step down and step away from full-time ministry in the local church. We assume there must be secret sin, a mental health breakdown, a lack of calling, or just plain failure. I was well aware of that stigma but too terrified to continue on with the way things were going.

"'I wish it need not have happened in my time,' said Frodo. 'So do I,' said Gandalf, 'and so do all who live to see such times. But that is not for them to decide. All we have to decide is what to do with the time that is given to us.'"[30]

Fearing for my emotional health and sanity more than perceived whispers and judgments from peers, I decided to leave the church and with it the only way of life I had ever known since being ordained in the early 2000s. Like Abraham,[31] my family went out, not knowing where we were going, how we were going to live, or what we were going to do. That decision would prove to be one of the best I had ever made, but it first ushered in an entire year of confusion, hurt, weakness, and waiting—always waiting. I had never realized how much of my life revolved around having something to look forward to until it was gone. Despite all our talk about the goodness of waiting on God, all waiting is not the same. Waiting to hear the doctor's prognosis about the growth she removed is different than waiting for a promotion at work. Waiting for a ride from a friend is different than waiting to see if anyone will show up to pick you up at the airport.

One kind of waiting requires patience; the other requires faith. We need patience when we're waiting for something to happen, but we need faith when we're not sure if anything is going to happen. Both are character building and lead to our good, but we don't experience them in the same way. The Apostle Paul describes how the earth waits with "eager longing" for the glory that will be revealed in the glorified church. He goes on to say three things: (1) the creation was subjected to frustration, (2) it is in bondage to decay, and 3) it groans with the pains of childbirth.[32] That's a pretty good description of waiting in faith. It's frustration, the feeling of

---

30. J. R. R. Tolkien, *The Fellowship of the Ring* (New York: Houghton Mifflin, 1954), 60.
31. See Heb. 11:8.
32. See Rom. 8:19–23.

bondage as time passes and waiting for the birth of something new, something to look forward to, something to center us again. Life in a fallen world brings trials that are designed by God to produce patient endurance, which leads to God's ultimate goal of producing in us maturity and character.[33]

As God forced me to wait, I could not reach for any of the familiar tools and weapons that had served me in the past. I knew enough to know that the strategies from the first half of life are insufficient to deal with the complexities of a crisis in the second half. The only way to deal with it was to walk through the experience entirely laid bare before the Lord and completely and admittedly vulnerable, weak, and powerless. This was the very thing my armor had been fashioned to protect me from my whole life. Recognizing our limits and shortcomings is a gift to and a problem for young leaders. In our youth, others begin to affirm our gifts and talents. Without the presence and voice of loving, honest, older, and wiser men and women in our lives, we live unaware that every ray of light in our lives also casts a shadow. Most of our positive attributes also have a negative side. We then lead and live for years with so much continuing affirmation that we may not be aware that we have a shadow side.

I have watched some leaders enter the second half of their lives and ministries and begin to focus on leadership skills, habits of highly effective people, or maximizing their potential to change the world. To be sure, there is nothing wrong with those pursuits, and they can lead to much human flourishing. But they can equally be the fig leaves we use to mask undesirable parts of ourselves and others. And in the final reckoning of our lives, the strategies we employ to feel better about our contribution to the world will have

---

33. See Rom. 5:3–5.

been seen as tools to delay the unavoidable approach of death. As youthful optimism succumbs to the inevitability of age, we must realize that laying down the idols of productivity and effectiveness is an invitation from Jesus to learn how to die. No matter how hard we train, our bodies are in decline on the slow path to inactivity. No matter how many crossword puzzles we do each day, our minds are becoming less focused and sharp than they once were. And at some point, the hope and thrill that came from looking forward will be replaced by some level of regret and sadness from looking back and realizing that not every dream came to pass.

God was gracious enough to orchestrate the circumstances of my life in such a way that I was forced to stare down the vilest parts of my soul. I previously had not wanted to admit they were there, much less examine them. I had to confront my mortality, my limits, my poor life choices, my shadows, and ultimately what I wanted the next 40 years of my life to look like should God be gracious to me. For a season, that decision helped me learn out of sheer necessity to live in the space between. I simply couldn't go back to what was, but I still had no idea of what was to come, much less what I hoped for in the coming years.

This liminal space is, by definition, a time of transition. At times, they are transitions we choose—a job transfer, moving to a new city, marriage, or perhaps a new child. These in-between spaces are strange for a season, but then we adjust to our lives being forever different.

At other times, these transitions are chosen for us. God may unmistakably shift the landscape of our lives and make it plain that a season of transition is coming, whether we welcome it or not. We may be tempted to shake our fist at the sky and blame God for the unwanted interruptions, roadblocks, or pain. There is a subtle grace when a loving, gracious Father is the one who chooses the environment and timing of our transitions. In my case, I would never have had the strength to willingly choose a liminal season and reevaluate the only way of living I had ever known. I would not have chosen to tear down my kingdom of self brick by brick. I would not have chosen to sit in the rubble and ashes of my previous life with only questions and no answers. But sometimes it is the kindness and severity of God to choose these things for us.[34] The prophet Jeremiah would not have chosen the rebellion and exile of the Jewish nation or the subsequent destruction of Jerusalem. He certainly did not want to sit in the debris of a destroyed city lamenting the former greatness, the brutal pillaging of the inhabitants, and the fact that God had allowed this suffering. Yet because of this, we have Jeremiah's words that bring comfort to those who are grieving. They show how God uses suffering in the lives of His children and reminds us that we are never alone no matter how desolate we feel.

Choosing Maturity

In a culture that primarily values success, fruitfulness, and onward movement, it is difficult to create space for the transitory periods of life that are full of awkwardness and mistakes. I have three sons, and I tried to intentionally create an initiation of sorts into young adulthood when they turned 13. Most cultures around the world have some sort of rite of passage when adulthood is intentionally conferred to children. There is typically some kind of difficulty to overcome, a measure of pain and discomfort, and some kind of instruction from elders. Most of these rites are also done when the child is completely naked, which makes sense to me. Any clothing, jewelry, or other marks of privilege or position

---

34. See Rom. 11:22.

in society are taken away, and the young man is left naked and defenseless. There may also be a first hunt with others or foraging for food and nourishment in the wilderness for a time. When they return to their village, they are accepted as men and expected to act like men. In some tribes, the women care for the younger boys. Around the time of the boys' 13th birthdays, the men of the tribe come into the village at night and "kidnap" their sons. The boys are blindfolded, stripped naked, taken into the bush to be circumcised, and left to fend for themselves for a season. Once the boys emerge from this process, they are reintroduced to the tribe as men.

It is instructive that we intuit the need to undress when facing some primal fear or challenge. We know that we must come just as we are and give ourselves over to someone or something greater than ourselves. All props are removed, and we have to lean into the sensation of being overwhelmed and underprepared. All of this makes the emergence of the young man the accomplishment it is.

Of course, I don't strip my children naked and leave them in a forest, but I do mark out space where they learn the responsibilities of adulthood from each important male figure in their lives. We sit around a table and share a meal. Afterward, each of the adult men shares something about becoming a man. Sometimes it is advice they wish they had received from their fathers or father figures. Other times, it is a word of wisdom they received from an older man in their lives. I also write a letter to each of my sons, read it to them, and then give it to them to keep. Then I take each son on a journey of their choice to spend one-on-one time together. I've always wanted to do a passport to purity type of thing, but my kids would mock something like that mercilessly (clearly we're a very spiritual family). Instead, I opt for something less scripted yet equally powerful—simple conversation. With one son, I taught him how to pray during an eight-hour drive to the mountains of Utah, using the Lord's Prayer as our template. For another, I engaged him in an equally long drive about discovering how our purpose in life is to give to and not take from those around us. We then discussed practical ways for a young man to be that kind of a presence in the lives of his friends and family.

We set up a welcome to adulthood by those who have been there. The ritual ushers in a space of transition for transformation. It is not a quick fix or immediately understood, but that is not the point. It is meant to help our children learn how to create and welcome a liminal space in their lives. These spaces (some would say *only* these spaces) demolish our self-constructed comfort zones and put us in an environment where we can begin to think, act, dream, and reimagine life in genuinely new ways. Liminal space is the ultimate teaching environment and something young men and women don't typically stumble upon without being taught the value of it.

Middle-aged men rarely welcome this space initially, but it proves necessary to shed the vestiges of things that once were true for new ways of being ourselves in the world. We reluctantly give up strategies that used to keep us safe, routines that used to comfort, narratives that used to keep us firmly in the role of the "good person." Our letting go enhances our ability to grasp what will be if we let it. That may be done volitionally or circumstantially—against our wishes. As Parker Palmer says, "We can use devastation as a seedbed for new life."[35] This is an exceptionally bitter pill to swallow for one who has done little

---

35. Parker J. Palmer, *A Hidden Wholeness: The Journey toward an Undivided Life* (San Francisco: Jossey-Bass, 2009), 5.

inner work to learn of the soul sustenance required to become the men and women God created us to be.

The good news of Jesus is that no steps to change are ever too little or any time too late to learn about our true selves in Christ. I have been comforted time and time again with the words of Isaiah that apply to the work of Jesus, that "a bruised reed he will not break, and a faintly burning wick he will not quench" (Isa. 42:3). It sounds too good to be true that my harsh inner critic is nothing like the Lord, and my self-condemnation does not have the final word over my life. And while this work can begin at any time in our lives, the outworkings of it do take time and effort for the rest of our lives. Maturity comes from learning to live in the tension with acceptance of both brokenness and wholeness in our lives. And that is enough work for any day.

LARVA

Emerging from the dark, shards of protective covering fall away.
All I know is hunger, and the name that they gave me.
Larva.
For such an ugly name, they tell me it means
I am not who I was yesterday, nor will be tomorrow.
All I know is hunger, and the name that they gave me.
Day by day, I grow comfortable with insatiable hunger and this ugly name,
Skin feeling itchy, bloated and uncomfortable,
Afraid of what this little death will bring.
Parts of me fall away, all to make room for what is underneath,
Always back to the voracious hunger, devouring everything around me.
Sometimes, it feels, including my own self
Layer after layer, formed, destroyed, and unformed
As I begin to become (so they tell me) what I one day will be
I just want this itching and hunger to stop and become this thing I'm not.

Φ

CHAPTER THREE: THE ROLE OF DISCIPLINE

Even though the fig trees have no blossoms,
and there are no grapes on the vines;
even though the olive crop fails,
    and the fields lie empty and barren;
even though the flocks die in the fields,
    and the cattle barns are empty,
yet I will rejoice in the Lord!
    I will be joyful in the God of my salvation!

—Hab. 3:17–18 NLT

At times there may be seasons of waiting that go hand in hand with the gracious discipline of our Father. While it can be difficult to know whether we are experiencing a specific discipline from God or the providence of waiting that comes to all, the way through it is not all that different. After all, times of waiting on God are a fertile time to do business with our inner lives. Even now, being disciplined sounds like a cold, unpleasant thing rather than the grace it actually is. The author of Hebrews reminds us of the purpose of discipline, calling it a "word of encouragement." He writes:

> *Do not make light of the Lord's discipline, and do not lose heart when he rebukes you, because the Lord disciplines the one he loves, and he chastens everyone he accepts as his son. No discipline seems pleasant at the time, but painful. Later on, however, it produces a harvest of righteousness and peace for those who have been trained by it.*
>
> —Heb. 12:5–6, 11 NIV

The experience of God's discipline is different from punishment, though it often feels the same. Punishment is punitive, meant to mete out the penalty for unjust actions. As followers of Jesus, we believe all our deserved punishment has been laid on Jesus Christ once and for all, and God has no need to punish an offense that has already been paid for by Jesus's death on the cross. Discipline is restorative, meant to teach us something we need to know in order to better inhabit God's world. Discipline is how God reminds us of His fatherhood. As the author of Hebrews says, "If you are left without discipline, in which all have participated, then you are illegitimate children and not sons" (Heb. 12:8). Regardless of the form discipline takes, we can welcome it as coming from the hand of a loving Father whose actions toward us are always for our good. Even in the painful process of waiting and discipline, God has embedded goodness.

Hebrews encourages us once more, "Therefore lift your drooping hands and strengthen your weak knees, and make straight paths for your feet, so that what is lame may not be put out of joint but rather be healed" (Heb. 12:12–13).

If discipline is restorative, meant to teach us how to better live in God's world, then surely it is meant to yield fruits of righteousness to those trained by it.[36] Rather than experiencing God as judge, examining our lives only to declare deficiency, would it not be more helpful to experience Jesus as an older brother who comes alongside us in our weakness to help expose some foolishness? Surely the most hardened and defensive among us are willing to admit that no one is perfect. Instead of using that imperfection as an excuse for sin, we can readily accept it as the truth that only God always does what is good, right, and perfect. Since I am not God, my lot is the same as all humanity—an imperfect sinner living by the grace of God, slowly being renewed through His Spirit. This is not truth to recoil from but to embrace. As imperfect as I am, change is possible because the same God who disciplines me desires to see that change as well.

In order to allow discipline to have its perfect work in us, we must embark on what some have called the inward journey. It requires digging underneath our actions to our motives and then under our motives to our fears. It requires brutal honesty with ourselves and a gospel big enough for us to hear the truth about ourselves and know we are still loved and accepted—not in spite of the truth about ourselves but because of it.

I am reminded of times when my children have done something foolish or hurtful and then try to cover it up with lies and half-truths. It grieves me as a father when they hide the truth from me, themselves, and God. But when one of my kids looks at me with fearful eyes and is brave enough to tell the truth, I melt. All

---

36. See Heb. 12:11.

my desire to wring the truth out of them is replaced with compassion and grace because now we can deal with the reality and see some healing and restoration. Without their confession, though, we are left only with delusion, wordplay, and circular arguments. It is impossible to convince someone of this if they are committed to deception. In this chapter, we'll talk more about the way this inward journey relates to emotional health and then come back to the idea of how it relates to discipline. This journey that uncovers dark parts of ourselves we would rather not deal with is ultimately good and leads to greater health and self-awareness.

So how do we begin? We start by acknowledging that each of us is full of light as well as shadow. We are capable of incredible sacrifice and selflessness as well as self-protection, deception, and selfishness. All aspects reside in the same soul, in one body. They are each true facets of ourselves, yet we are still malleable. What is currently true of us does not have the power to define us for all time, not when Jesus is always present and we are in Him. It is similar to the way statistics define the truth of the past but have no power to dictate the reality of the future. Being disciplined actually helps us narrow down the shadows and identify which aspect we can bring into the light of God's truth in order to seek healing. If you suspect you are being disciplined, it is never for the kinds of weakness common to humanity—wandering thoughts that need to be taken captive, errant desires that are felt and then dismissed, or impure motives we are able to identify quickly and then change course. God may be disciplining us to uncover one area we are probably already aware of.

Take a good look at your life. How are you spending your time, energy, and money? What thoughts consistently dominate the landscape of your mind, and what feelings does your heart gravitate to, knowing full well there is death down that road? You likely have one behavior, character trait, or impure desire that is not leading to life and peace. It may be an unhealthy addiction to social media, sex, entertainment, your phone, or anything else you use to numb yourself. It may be a constant abrasiveness or defensiveness with those around you. It may be relational drama that always seems to follow you for some reason, evidenced in unhealthy relationships, discord, and strife. Whatever it is, if it is something consistent enough to merit the discipline of a loving Father, you are likely aware of it already or can be with some quiet reflection.

Greater emotional health comes by asking good questions about these areas of your life. By using the framework of inductive Bible study methodology through observation, interpretation, and application, we have a trellis to begin building on. Observation means paying attention to what we are seeing, feeling, or experiencing. Interpreting those observations leads to asking why we are feeling, thinking, or acting the way we are. Application is where we bring the gospel of Jesus to bear on those truths about ourselves.

Observation

First, paying attention to our emotions can unearth existing areas we need to change or grow in. By paying attention, I don't mean thinking about it while you are reading this book. This level of work requires us to budget time for silence and solitude through which we hear the Word of God. Find a quiet spot where you can be alone and unbothered for several minutes, and then prayerfully ask yourself some of these questions:

- Where is there brokenness in my life?
- Where is there guilt or shame?

- What accomplishment am I most proud of right now? Why?
- What am I most afraid of right now?
- What do I most look forward to doing or experiencing?
- Where am I feeling hopelessness?
- What am I most anxious about?
- What causes the most frustration in my life?
- What is currently bringing me the most joy or excitement?
- Are there any people in my life I am currently avoiding? Why?
- Are there any people I look forward to seeing?
- What relationships are the most life-giving to me? Why?
- Which relationships are the most emotionally draining? Why?

Interpretation

The answers to all those questions are ripe for examination, uncovering the first layer of our lives, the most easily identifiable parts of our thoughts and actions. You may be unaware of why you feel a certain way (excited, anxious, fearful), but bringing understanding and insight is the job of the Holy Spirit, our Counselor. Once we observe the truth about how we feel, we can bring that to God in prayer and ask Him to reveal ourselves to ourselves.

Next, we dig deeper to identify the motivations behind our actions. Perhaps the person you most look forward to seeing is a man or a woman who is not your spouse. By asking yourself to be honest about why you feel that way, you find that they make you feel desirable, intelligent, or caring. Honest answers then allow you to begin asking a different set of questions. Why does this person's opinion of me matter so much? What am I deriving from this person or relationship? To spin out another set of questions, maybe you find you are anxious about performing well at work, which is a perfectly good desire. You start asking more questions about your work and find that while you consistently excel at every project or task you are given, you always feel anxious about the next one. You might realize there is some scenario from your past when, in spite of your best efforts, you were not able to perform well, and you are afraid that might happen again. Or maybe you become aware of the amount of talk among coworkers of budget cuts and impending downsizing and find you are actually living in fear of losing your job.

Application

Now that you have uncovered some latent emotions just underneath the surface of your life, you can do some true inner work on your journey. Applying wisdom to the perceived interpretations of our life experiences may come through several practices. The first one is simply telling your story to another person. That may be telling your life story, telling the story of your day, or telling the story of a specific incident that triggered this awareness. It is impossible to overstate the importance of being completely and totally relational. A desire and capacity for relationship with God, self, and others is bound up in the DNA of God's universe as a reflection of the trinitarian community of Father, Son, and Spirit. As Rich Plass and Jim Cofield say in their excellent book *The Relational Soul*, "God designed us to be *for* another. God designed us to receive *from* another. We even receive our understanding of our self in relationship with another. . . . Because we bear God's relational likeness, we can commune with God. We also have the capability of connecting with each other in mutually self-flourishing ways."[37]

---

37. Rich Plass and Jim Cofield, *The Relational Soul: Moving from False Self to Deep Connection* (Downers Grove, IL: IVP Books, 2014), 13.

Nothing about our understanding of God from Scripture would lead us to believe it is possible to live a healthy, enjoyable life apart from healthy, enjoyable relationships. Plass and Cofield also state, "Our relationships determine whether we have and enjoy life. Relational connection is that profound and that necessary. It is that basic."[38]

The relational nature of reality is wrapped up in the ancient Ignatian practice of paying attention to consolations and desolations. Consolations are those moments in our lives when we are moving toward God, aware of His presence, and enjoying a relationship with Him. Desolations are those moments when we are moving away from God and frequently accompanied by resentment, envy, doubt, shame, and so on. As a daily practice, it is a helpful way to begin to first observe where we were during the day and then interpret those observations. My family began doing this together on Sunday mornings during the 2020 quarantine. After gathering for teaching and music (online in our living room), we shared about moments that week when we felt close or far from God. It was a great way to reconnect as a family while leading our children in a practice of honesty and grace.

Another way to apply the truth of the gospel is to find a friend who is both a good listener and able to hold your story with grace and gentleness. That's a great gift and a topic worthy of an entire book. If you don't currently have relationships like that, you can begin developing your own skill set by listening to others well with the ability to hold their story in confidence and without judgment. You may also want to start by seeking out a spiritual director, a trusted leader, or a therapist to learn how it

---

38. Plass and Cofield, *The Relational Soul*, 13.

feels to be able to share your story in an appropriate and healthy way. Another way to apply these truths comes from a counselor friend of mine[39] who has helped me make sense of my story. She asked me to fix my mind on a situation that happened recently. It was typically a disturbing incident or something that revealed a part of myself I wished weren't true. I remembered the questions she asked by the acronym TINNS, which stands for nothing more than a device to remember it by.

> *Trigger:* Did anything set you off? What about this incident brought up negative feelings or emotions? What was the event that started a chain reaction?
>
> *Image:* What mental picture defines the worst part of that memory? What image comes to mind as you remember this situation?
>
> *Negative Belief:* What is the false belief about yourself? What is true about yourself? What would you like to be true about yourself?
>
> *Negative Emotion:* How does that negative belief make you feel? What does it make you feel about yourself (be as specific as possible)?
>
> *Sensation:* Where do you feel your response in your body? Is it a tightness in your chest? A rapid heart rate? Something you intuit in your gut?

After walking me through this exercise, she asked me how negative my reaction was on a scale of 1 to 7 and then asked what was keeping it at that number. What might I do to lower the number?

---

39. I am indebted to Amy Karman, LMFT, for this insight and for being the first person to help me process my story.

Once we identify how we are experiencing these events in our minds, bodies, and emotions, we can take a step back from the triggering incident to ask deeper questions about where our reactions are coming from.

How does this inward journey relate to discipline? When we become aware of experiencing the discipline of God, there is always the external behavior or action—the tip of the iceberg, so to speak—and all the factors and causes for that behavior that exist under the surface. True redemptive change happens when we follow our behavior to the underlying fears, anxieties, and negative beliefs about ourselves, others, and God. Once we have looked into what is really going on in our souls, we can bring to Jesus the truth about why we do what we do. He is not afraid of what you just found. He is not embarrassed of your shameful secrets, and He is certainly not looking to make pronouncements of truth over your lies in a way that demeans you. The Father who disciplines every child is seen clearly in Jesus, and we are told that "He will not crush the weakest reed or put out a flickering candle" (Matt. 12:20 NLT). Rather, He nurtures what is broken by binding it and cups the flame against the wind until it burns brightly once again.

I have found many of the sinful behaviors that hurt me and others have at their core a wound I received in the past that I have not acknowledged, worked through, and brought to Jesus to heal. The Apostle Paul tells the church in Thessalonica how to deal with others gently, taking their own stories into account. "Warn those who are lazy. Encourage those who are timid. Take tender care of those who are weak. Be patient with everyone" (1 Thess. 5:14 NLT). Notice that only the intentionally lazy are strongly warned while the rest are encouraged and cared for. If this is our counsel for how to treat each other, how much more is it true of how God treats us?

This all serves to frame discipline in a more hopeful, positive light. Who doesn't want greater health, clarity, and freedom? And whether it was discipline that led to a season of liminality as we worked through it or a season of waiting that slowed us down enough to see areas where God was discipling us, we can thank Him for the space between.

Φ

CHAPTER FOUR:
EMOTIONAL HEALTH

I think age is a very high price to pay for maturity.
—Tom Stoppard

As far as you can, hold your confidence.
Do not allow your confusion to squander
This call which is loosening
Your roots in false ground,
That you might come free
From all you have outgrown.

What is being transfigured here is your mind,
And it is difficult and slow to become new.
The more faithfully you can endure here,
The more refined your heart will become
For your arrival in the new dawn.
—John O'Donohue, "For the Interim Time"

Being and Doing

The experience of liminality is a necessary step on the journey from disproportionately valuing doing instead of being. Many have tried to assess the different stages and seasons of our lives, and there is great value in looking at the broad strokes of your life to unearth patterns and commonalities. When speaking of this, Franciscan author Father Richard Rohr says, "There are two major tasks in the human spiritual journey. The task of the first half of life is to create a proper *container* for one's life and answer some central questions. 'Who Am I?' 'What makes me significant?' 'How can I support myself?' 'Who will go with me?'"[40] He goes on to describe these developmental tasks as identity, boundaries, law, structure, and authority. "The task of the second half of life is, quite simply, to find the actual *contents* that this container was meant to hold and deliver. In other words, the container is for the sake of the contents."[41]

For those with my same temperament—one of action, productivity, and efficiency—doing is a means of creating Rohr's container. Who am I? I am a pastor. I am a husband. I am a father. What makes me significant? My output. My teaching. My service to others. While being a beloved son of God adopted through the finished work of Jesus Christ is the truest thing about me, it's hard to compete with the dose of self-worth that comes from exceptional performance. There is something satisfying in the short term about feeling like you have made a meaningful contribution to the world through personal effort. It feels good to feel strong, capable, and independent. Yet how does a student of Jesus move through life prizing strength when our weakness is

---

40. Richard Rohr, *Falling Upward: A Spirituality for the Two Halves of Life* (San Francisco, CA: Jossey-Bass, 2011), 1.
41. Ibid.

the path to His strength?[42] How can we prize our competence when grace (unmerited favor) is the reason for anything we do?[43] How can we feign independence when a primary mark of a disciple is dependence on God alone? Surely our doing must be in service to something bigger and truer than ourselves.

Czech author Milan Kundera writes, "I was not a hypocrite, with one real face and several false ones. I had several faces because I was young and didn't know who I was or wanted to be."[44] This first half of life brings out all the faces we may wear for a given time to find which one works best in order to accomplish our goals. Which one keeps me hidden? Which one gets me noticed? Which one keeps me safe? Who do I need to be in order to live the good life? What we can't know in the ignorance of our youth is the violence all this does to our soul. Wearing these masks, either real or imagined, allows us to form an identity (Rohr's container) without ever knowing what that identity was meant to support in the first place. We build the nicest containers, the newest containers, the slimmest containers, the brightest and loudest containers, and the smartest containers, and then we step back to pride ourselves in our abilities and competencies without ever asking what the goal was in the first place.

Self-Awareness Is Not Enough

Emotional health is the fruit of coming to terms with the person we currently are, both light and shadow. Unlike spiritual maturity, biblical orthodoxy, or mental acuity, emotional intelligence is much earthier. It refers to our ability to intuit what is going on

---

42. See 2 Cor. 12:9–10.
43. See 1 Cor. 15:10.
44. Milan Kundera, *The Joke* (New York: Harper Perennial, 1993), 33.

inside of us and why it is happening, as well as understanding the same regarding others. Self-awareness is a central feature of emotional health since it gives us a tool to recognize our own emotions in the moment and the potential effects they have on us and others. Yet self-awareness without change and real transformation won't produce lasting health.

To awareness, we add regulation, the process whereby we take those emotions captive to the obedience of Christ. Rather than being driven by unchecked emotions and feelings, we recognize what they are and where they come from. We can learn to welcome those emotions into our lives without letting them drive the car. Since we are unable to get rid of all negative thoughts and emotions for good, the best we can do is pay attention to them and regulate their effects by being firmly in control of them. As we grow in regulating these emotions, we learn to take responsibility for ourselves, regardless of external stimuli (others are not responsible for why we do what we do). We become more flexible and able to handle change, disruption, and new information with grace, as well as create an allowance for failure in ourselves and those around us.

As we begin to experience greater freedom from anxiety, shame, and fear by paying attention to them, we become more motivated to pay attention to the way these emotions are at play in others, both to help them regulate and to teach ourselves a healthy separation—we are not responsible for what others do and why they do it. This leads to all kinds of empathetic connection we may have found difficult before. When we don't take responsibility for the behavior of others, we become more in tune with the social signals they give off, as well as our own. We begin to anticipate how others might be feeling in a way that leads us to proceed with both gentleness and caution toward them. We become leaders who empower others to do their own inner work in order to excel in their lives. We can better manage the power dynamics of working with a team, from the vocally anxious team member who holds influence because they introduce fear and worry to the quiet innovator who needs to be asked to speak and will not fight to be heard among louder personalities.

As we learn these skills, we develop another tool—the ability to truly understand others by discerning the impact their past has on their present, whether they realize it or not. To illustrate this idea, I'll share a time when I was working closely with a leader who had been raised by a single mother after her father walked out when she was two years old. She never mentioned her father, never talked about her feelings toward him, and was very thankful for the mother who chose to stay around and do the hard work of raising children by herself. I was not mature or aware enough at the time to recognize that someone orphaned by a primary male influence in their life is bound to have difficulty relating to a father figure, an older man, or someone who feels parental. I was also unaware of how that was sure to spill over into her relationship with me, her direct supervisor. Again, without taking responsibility, we can be responsive toward others' stories while maintaining our own personal health and boundaries.

These are all pieces of our emotional intelligence (EI). Since they are so fundamental to successful relationships, creative partnerships, and potentially divisive communities, why do they come so difficult and so late for some of us? How could we possibly lead without them? Once again, the liminal space created by the ending of something valuable to us and the unknown future gives us time to pay attention to the things we were too busy to pay attention to. This attention is one of the greatest gifts of the space between. While we like to think that we are moderately aware individuals who are paying attention to our lives, much of our behavior comes from a place of implicit memory, the things we remember unconsciously and effortlessly, things we don't have to make a concentrated effort to recall. Skills like reading, driving, and walking are implicit. And implicit memories can involve ways of thinking about ourselves and relating to others. If we don't need to make an effort for things that come implicitly, what else are we not paying attention to simply because it's always been that way? Dr. Curt Thompson refers to the experiments that have been done to identify the parts of our brain responsible for paying attention. He says, "The brain is constantly filtering dozens of stimuli, enabling us to focus on some things while eliminating others from the mind's view. . . . To what will you lend your most focused attention?" He summarizes by asking, *"How well am I paying attention to what I am paying attention to?"*[45]

While everyone has a different story and background with different emotional contours and physiological baggage, there are some commonalities I have experienced myself and seen in other leaders that contribute to the challenge of growing in this area.

I recently heard of a consultant who asked a group of pastors and leaders, "Outside of your spouse, is there a single person you have a full disclosure kind of relationship with? One person that you do not filter your words or manage your image with. Just pure truth about everything going on inside of you."[46] After spending time with various leaders in different areas, he found that about 70 percent of them did not have any vulnerable relationships with someone other than their spouse. Think about the level of emotional intelligence a pastor must develop to grow into the role of shepherd. The level of awareness needed to deal with an entire congregation who likely would never have found each other if not

---

45. Curt Thompson, *Anatomy of the Soul* (Carol Stream, IL: Tyndale House Publishers, 2010), 52, 53.
46. Henry Cloud, interview on the podcast *Managing Leadership Anxiety,* S5 E1.

for their common faith in Jesus is substantial. When does this lack of vulnerability begin? And given the problematic consistency of moral failure among religious leaders, what kind of system consistently produces that statistic of 70 percent?

My story is similar to most young leaders, at least among my peer relationships with pastors. When I began my ministry career, I was young, gifted, and insecure. Two of those things seemed like a liability to accomplishing what I hoped as a pastor. Naturally, we gravitate toward the tools that help us mitigate our perceived liability. Over time, the overt emphasis of our gifts without a concurrent assessment of our limitations becomes cemented into our worldview and our perception of ourselves and others. If we are not cautious, it can become something we weaponize. We do not tolerate weakness in ourselves and others. We do not make allowances for the limitations of others. We can become so familiar with pushing ourselves to the brink of exhaustion that we expect the same from everyone around us. Others who do have healthy and appropriate boundaries are told that they are not being team players. Self-awareness is a start, but without self-compassion it can be little more than harsh condemnation.

When we can show grace to the worst aspects of ourselves while being compassionate with our own failings, then the real work of self-awareness—transformation—begins. It is common for young leaders with substantial gifts to quickly find themselves in situations they simply don't have the character to sustain. Over time, they find that they are older than they once were with gifts more finely honed and intuitive, but they still haven't compensated for their nagging sense of inadequacy. Every self-development conference boasts key-note messages from pastors of large churches or organizations (bigger is better). Everything being celebrated is loud and dramatic (the show matters). The stories we tell and the things we marvel at are things that happen to other people more quickly than they happen to us (rapid growth is standard). We are captivated by pastors in our Instagram feeds who are full of capacity, competency, great insight, and confidence (strength is preferable to weakness).

What other value but exceptionalism could a young leader possibly walk away with from living in such an environment? And perhaps more poignantly, how did a Western expression of Christianity come to embrace the antithesis of everything true about the way of Jesus? The Bible tells us that the way of Jesus is small, not large, like a mustard seed that grows and grows. The way of Jesus is quiet, not loud, like roots growing unseen underground with no discernible fruit. The way of Jesus is slow, not fast, like the parable of the weeds and the wheat growing together until harvest. The way of Jesus is weak, not strong, like the crazy prophets the world was not worthy to receive. The way of Jesus seems foolish, not wise, like walking around a fortified city seven times to defeat a better-trained army.

It's no wonder character seems so blasé considering the spectacular things we could be doing, celebrating, or working toward. It also shouldn't surprise anyone that for all our learning in seminary, this was one lesson we knew in concept but not in practice.

Delusion and Diligence

Another difficulty lies in the trap of self-protection that leads to self-delusion. Activity allows us to mentally check out from our inner lives in a way that can divorce us from the hard work of actually abiding in Jesus. We know that apart from Him, we can do nothing, so we convince ourselves that we are partners with the Savior in our life's work. By doing so, we can easily forget that the work of sanctification is not tremendously different from God's work of justification. We believe we have been saved by grace through faith. Then somewhere down the line, we believe that the impetus for change is up to us. Yet the very grace that first birthed life in our souls is the same grace that teaches our souls to continue to find rest in God alone.[47] God can only work with the reality of things we have allowed to define us, which requires a brutal honesty with those things. And here is the thing: no one has ever come to a deeper knowledge of self while on the go. Read that again. No one. At best, Jesus may bring to mind thoughts we file away to do business with later, but the environment of stillness, solitude, and silence are the only fertile soil in which to grow a healthy branch attached to the True Vine. Thus, the experience of waiting comes one way or another.

Some time ago, my doctor gave me a particular antibiotic for an infection I had. I dutifully took the drug every day, even as my body started to develop a rash and my bodily functions began to shut down. I couldn't eat, sleep, or go to the bathroom for several days, yet I kept taking the medicine. After a sleepless Saturday night, I was deciding whether to preach the next morning since I have an unmerited amount of confidence in my own ability. One of my elders told me to stay home and that he would take over for me. My wife decided enough was enough and took me to the emergency room where I discovered I was allergic to the sulfa drug, my body was close to sepsis, and it was, in fact, shutting down. Dehydrated, weak, and so, so tired, I left the hospital under orders to rest in bed for two weeks while my body regained strength.

During the two weeks in bed with little to no strength to get much of anything done between naps, I had a lot of time to wait on God. As I was slowly gaining enough strength to take a shower and get dressed, I still felt functionally useless, watching life happen all around me. The only task on my to-do list was to rest and get

---

47. See Ps. 62:5.

healthy. God used that time to show me some ugly things about myself and my own need to feel needed. The church went on as normal, my family continued to function, and God somehow kept the world spinning in spite of my incapacitation. Why was I so afraid to do what I needed to get better? What did I think would happen if I couldn't perform? Being practically bedridden certainly made life more difficult for those around me (in part because I'm a big baby when I'm sick), but they loved me well and picked up any slack. I was left with a lot of silence and stillness in which I was able to hear God better. Whether we are choosing to wait on God or being forced to, He knows how to get our attention and will go to great lengths to be what we need when we need it. A friend of mine says that God continually offers us invitations to be with Him, but if we refuse those invitations, He knows how to hamstring and sideline us. I needed to face the facts that I have limits and that I am my own worst enemy when it comes to recognizing and making allowance for them. I would like to think I would listen to my body more quickly now than I did then, but I know myself too well. I still have a long way to go. The only difference is that now I can appreciate the value of the dry times of waiting. Like the prophet Habakkuk, I now know that even though the fig tree does not blossom and fruit is not on the vine, it is possible to rejoice in the Lord, taking joy in the God of my salvation.[48]

The opposite of self-deception and delusion is diligence. It means not only paying attention to what we're paying attention to but actually doing something about it. I have benefited greatly from the work of Murray Bowen, a scholar, psychiatrist, clinician, teacher, and counselor. He developed the family systems theory, a way of viewing our family of origin as a social system

---

48. See Hab. 3:18.

that influences our behavior. Complementary to a genogram, it helps us appreciate the interconnectedness that shapes our behavior that stems from our families. The theory is that by knowing how the emotional system in our family works, we gain a greater appreciation for each other's weaknesses and strengths and develop better strategies for problem-solving by identifying deeply ingrained and conditioned patterns of behavior.

Bowen identified eight concepts that frame his thinking about families and have been incredibly beneficial in my own emotional health work. Of course, if the family is viewed as a primary social structure that shapes our behavior, it's no surprise the church is family 2.0. We each bring our own upbringings, assumptions, family cultures, and ways of relating to each other into the church, affecting every relationship we have. All relational patterns that developed in us early on are coping mechanisms for us to manage the anxieties of life and relationships. By paying attention to these patterns, we can better engage relationally with others. This engagement can come through understanding what environments produce the most anxiety in us and how to remain deeply connected to others without sacrificing our autonomy (differentiation). It also comes through understanding our patterns of managing stress, conflict, or emotional distancing (nuclear family emotional process) and how our insecurities can affect our parenting (multigenerational transmission process).

Emotional intelligence is not something we gain simply by listening to a podcast or reading a book. It is the fruit of living in community and practicing how we relate to one another. Adding diligence of practice to our self-awareness helps make us a better lover of God and people. The ability to pursue these things in the midst of our own waiting and confusion is the fruit of maturity.

C T R I L R
A E P L A

Gradually familiarity comes with this new body, new skin, and new name
They tell me I will be Monarch! A Queen! A Ruler!
And though all I can see is lumpy flesh, too many legs, and sharp teeth
I am adored by people everywhere, going out of their way to neither crush
nor harm me
Seemingly knowing something I have yet to discover.
I gladly walk on fingertips of loving children
Rapt with attention to every detailed part
Gently appreciating my beauty
And I, in turn, let them
Basking in their appreciation of me.
Why did no one tell me how good this would be?
This caterpillar is superior to the larva that was once small and ugly
but now affirmed as distinctive and unique
Yet still . . . the unquenchable hunger remains.
These eight legs are now a joy, and how perfect these sharp teeth are for
eating leaves!
This silk helps clothe and warm the adoring children
They tell me that only my silk is considered good
enough for Kings and Queens
Just as I myself now am.
Still this cycle of never-ending hunger that no leaf seems to satisfy
The silk I spin is little comfort, and does nothing to take the ache
I would gladly give up the adoring eyes for just one day of contentment.
And as I now have to deal with the source of this hunger
They tell me something more to come
Death! Disintegration! Darkness!
But all I know is fatigue, heaviness, and this insatiable appetite.
Tired of these new names, tired of the craving, tired of myself
The weight has become too much to bear
I would gladly give all that I am for a safe comfortable place to hide in
Just for a while.
So I employ the one thing I own and can use
Silk: this seemingly frail, thin fiber
But I know, strong enough to hold this tired body of mine.
So close, so full, so tired, I just need some rest
And now it's almost done, the darkness closes in and I . . .

Φ

CHAPTER FIVE:
CRUCIBLES AND
CREATIVITY

If we can't embrace the whole of who we are—
embrace it with transformative love—we'll imprison
the creative energies hidden in our own shadows
and be unable to engage creatively with the world's
complex mix of shadow and light.

—Parker Palmer

Shadows and Light

To appreciate the complexity of our makeup as human beings, we need creativity. Far from being the sole tool of artists, creativity is how we all learn to envision a different future. The ability to produce something new comes from the ability to imagine something new, which comes from a desire for something new, different, or better. The seeming barrenness of in-between spaces is often the ideal environment to envision some kind of change. One of the ways creativity flourishes during seasons of transition is illustrated by the concept of negative space. It is a technique where artists use not just the subject but the area around and between an image in order to draw attention to itself rather than the image. Just because the space might be bare, there is still power in the shadows. By removing the main element of an image, we can evoke mystery, longing, and ironically call attention to the larger meaning behind the work.[49]

The concept of portraying substance by using open space is why negative space has so much power. Negative space is made up of actual shapes that share edges with the positive space. Learning to see and appreciate negative spaces requires learning to see in a new or abstract way. This is true of art and even truer of our lives. Consider the use of negative space in music. Sometimes it's an unexpected beat of silence before the chorus drops that creates tension before catharsis; other times it is an intentionally placed ambient interlude. Sometimes it's a relaxing tempo to rest from the driving force of the entire song. Or maybe it's a way of using sound as an invitation to contemplate and reflect on the music and the emotions it elicits. All of this points to the same truth: a well-timed pause helps bring clarity, definition, and impact to both the silence and the music. In our lives, periods of waiting create the needed negative space in order to produce something new, reimagine something familiar, or be the catalyst for some other change.

Learning to view life through a new or potentially abstract lens may at first be disorienting but ultimately pushes us to abide in Jesus as our centering truth and reality. Total dependence

---

49. One of the most popular examples of this is Rubin's vase. Google it.

on Jesus as our so-called north star in life and ministry means abiding—or living—in Him as we come to know the truth that sets us free from binary either-or thought patterns.[50]

Even if we were capable of always being at our best, it would still be insufficient to display the multifaceted creativity for which God made us. We are not two-dimensional creatures, choosing good or bad, light or darkness; rather, we are full-orbed, dimensional creatures who exist in both the light and the darkness. As Martin Luther famously wrote, *"Simul justus et peccator"* ("Simultaneously justified and sinner"). We embody both the shadow and the light because we are full of both shadows and light. To the degree that we understand the complexity with which we've been created, we are able to truly image the manifold wisdom of God.[51]

Learning to live with the tension that comes from two competing truths creates a cognitive and emotional dissonance. We can become so used to binary thinking that we have a hard time reconciling that two different things may, in fact, be true at the same time. For instance, I believe I am good at my job. This is a positive belief that allows me to feel good about myself as a man, an employer, a provider for my family, and a gifted individual doing good work. It is equally true that I make mistakes at my job. Sometimes they are harmless omissions where I simply forget to do something promised. Other times, there is internal anxiety or tension that spills out in my leadership to other people and could have been better managed. Finally, there are times when my own brokenness and wounds cause real hurt and pain that require recognition, repentance, and restoration. I now have two things that

---

50. See John 8:31.
51. See Eph. 3:9–10.

are equally true in a both-and world but cannot be reconciled in an either-or worldview. If I need to believe I am so good at my job that I never make mistakes, I will not be able to acquiesce to this reality, pushing one truth away to more easily believe the other. If I believe that making mistakes means I am not good at my job, I will do my best to deny any error. And so, we see the power of "and."[52] I am good at my job *and* I am capable of making mistakes. I am a hard worker *and* I can procrastinate and be incredibly lazy. I am deeply loving *and* deeply selfish. I am faithful *and* I am prone to wander. All these are true simultaneously, and there is freedom in that recognition.

Endless Possibilities

I have a confession. I strongly dislike contemporary Christian music. It often chooses to communicate what is right doctrinally rather than the messier emotions of what is real experientially. Other times, it can become a cheap facsimile of the work of others who deal with the same topics or subjects with greater honesty and depth. In the late 1990s, there were posters that categorized Christian music into a genre with the heading "For fans of . . ." I'm certainly not opposed to Christians making music in a genre I already like, but I am opposed to presenting it as a safe alternative to those other bad guys. A popular local Christian radio station advertises itself as "safe for the whole family." What that means practically is that the station predominantly plays music from artists who work with safe emotions—joy, love, peace, patience, kindness, goodness. There are no imprecatory songs wishing

---

52. Jim Herrington and Trisha Taylor, "The Power of 'And,'" August 13, 2020, in *The Leaders Journey*, podcast, 28:08, https://theleadersjourney.us/ep44/.

death and dismemberment on enemies.[53] There's also no talk of sin that continues to entangle when we are not experiencing victory. And certainly there are no songs that question God's goodness and sound more like an angry shouting match at heaven while God remains silent.

This is curious for music ostensibly about "a man of sorrows and acquainted with grief" or a man who had no beauty that we would desire him and was despised, rejected, oppressed, smitten by God, and afflicted.[54] If anyone knows the pain of loneliness, the sting of betrayal, and unjust suffering, it is Jesus Christ, Son of God, Savior. Surely this gives us permission to also feel these things and learn how to suffer well. Yet often in a culture that celebrates victory and exceptionalism, we don't know how to lament well, if at all. We rush past the darkness to get back to His marvelous light and lose the ability to identify with those who have long sat in darkness without the opportunity to see any light.[55] It is true that Jesus is a light that shines in dark places, but it is precisely because of the totality of the darkness that the light can be seen so greatly. If Christ is truly light for the life of the world,[56] then surely He must have something to say to the darkness and those who dwell in it. How else would the light appear more desirable than the familiarity of the shadow of death?

The same Jesus who died on the cross experienced the worst evils of humanity that were placed on His perfect soul and then spent three days in Sheol before rising from the dead. Romans 1:4 says Jesus was declared to be the Son of God in power only through His resurrection from the dead. His life and experience

---

53. See Ps. 137:9.
54. See Isa. 53:1–10.
55. See 1 Pet. 2:9, Matt. 4:15–16.
56. See John 6:33.

allowed Him to fully identify with us (light and shadow), and His descent into Sheol allowed Him to fully confront evil. His resurrection was the declaration of His power over all things, both in heaven, on earth, and under the earth.[57]

When Jesus experienced all this darkness in the world, it was not revolutionary or new. He came from a long line of Jewish men and women who also lived, wrote about, and worshipped God through those shadowy emotions. Throughout the Bible, we are confronted with unsafe people, places, and situations that would make our Christian radio station blush. It is good and right to focus on the more victorious and celebratory aspects of our faith—overcoming the world by the blood of the Lamb and our testimony,[58] being given a spirit of power, love, and a sound mind instead of fear,[59] and singing songs of celebration and thanksgiving.[60] But we must not imbalance the scales so that praise and power are the only parts of Scripture that receive attention from our pulpits, artists, conferences, magazines, and books.

Creativity is an integral part of God's character and nature. Not only does it help us imagine a better, healthier future for ourselves, but it helps us hold the tension of differing truths that currently exist. The greatest gift of artists to society is the ability to portray truth in a striking way through a variety of mediums. Artists take what scientists classify and systematize and bring the same truth in a way that cuts our hearts as well as our minds. One of the things that strikes me about all my artist friends is their desire to create something true for themselves, unconcerned with using any existing categories for their work as long as it

---

57. See Phil. 2:10.
58. See Rev. 12:11.
59. See 2 Tim. 1:7.
60. See Jer. 30:19.

communicates something near to their hearts. As a digression, close to the time of this writing, the biggest hit of the year was Lil Nas X's "Old Town Road." It was a genre-defying song that was played repeatedly and became ubiquitous. An article in the *Los Angeles Times* discussed how some country music fans were upset about the cultural appropriation of their music. What struck me about that article is that it felt like a decades-old argument most people don't believe anymore. Without further digressing about the history of how musicians have always played with genre norms of the time, it is a positive development that we don't trap our most creative citizens inside a box created to be easily understood, packaged, marketed, and sold to the masses. The dynamic explosion of distribution methods this decade also contributes to artists being able to authentically create something true for them and then distribute it to a wider audience who won't likely encounter them on the top-40 radio stations.

One of my favorite artists in the last few years is a young band from Flagstaff called Tow'rs. What I love about their music is the real and raw exploration of experiences common to mankind yet with a poetic flourish incredibly satisfying to me. One of their songs, "Vanilla Pines," beautifully captures the experience of a relationship between two people who are constantly changing and allowing room for that kind of growth without boxing each other in to who they used to be. "Let's light this house on fire, four walls hold us no longer, we dance in the warmth of its blaze, stand tall like vanilla pines, every day is another try to choose to do more than survive, *We could do more than survive.*"[61] Having been married for 20 years, I know this to be true. My wife and I are not the same people we married, and there is something about

---

61. "Vanilla Pines," track 3 on Tow'rs, *Tow'rs*, 2014.

the medium of song for me that takes a truth like that and makes it explode in my heart as well as my mind.

Creatives are a God-given gift to the rest of the community, creating awe, wonder, and worship. God doesn't give creative gifts just for explicitly religious art, but in the book of Exodus, He chose two creative men for the work of building the temple. Bezalel and his assistant, Oholiab, (1) were chosen by name and commissioned to create furnishings and relics for the temple and the people, (2) were filled with His Spirit for the ability to create, (3) were given the ability to work with gold, silver, and bronze,[62] carving and engraving wood and mounting gemstones, and (4) were given great wisdom to accomplish the commission. That's a lot of attention and detail on God's part just to make some forks, knives, and anointing oil. Even in the ordinary, creatives can imbue their work with a transcendence that comes from the crucible of their own lives.

Renewed Creativity

Artist Makoto Fujimura first introduced me to the Nihonga (Japanese) style of painting. What distinguishes Nihonga from Western oil-based paintings is the materials. The materials must come from a process of the death of something. They require considerable time to make and more time to create with them. The silk canvas is an exceptional material to paint since it allows a variety of effects to the color. It is made from the silk of the *Bombyx mori*, a caterpillar that turns into a moth. The cocoon, the instrument of death and rebirth, is placed into hot water to unravel the long strands of silk that are used for the canvas. The pigments used for painting, called iwa-enogu, are produced by grinding natural minerals. After the crushing process, some are

---

62. See Exod. 31:1–11.

roasted in fire to produce variations in color. Since the pigments have no natural adhesive properties, the painting is coated in nikawa, a gelatin made from boiling and extracting protein from the dead bodies of animals and fish. Much death is required to create the materials used to bring something new into the world. Life imitates art, and vice versa.

I am convinced that every creative endeavor that deals honestly with shadows came from a confusing time of waiting. Even seeds planted in the soil of pain and watered with our own tears can produce a life-giving tree of joy.[63] When we are forced to sit and linger with our misplaced affections, the bitterness of that experience can become sweet when we see where it leads. Waiting often puts us in the position of having to recognize the source of our pain. If we are being honest with ourselves, we may start with fingers pointed at everyone and everything around us, including (or especially) God, but in the end, we're still left with our own contribution to the problem.

Creativity comes from being aware long enough to sit in sackcloth and ashes with more questions than answers and more anger than peace. Dealing with our shadow side can unlock new perspectives of ourselves and the world around us. If we try to only be our best selves, we will forget reality—that we are full-orbed, four-dimensional creatures who exist in the light, the darkness, and a lot of shades of gray. We embody both the shadow and the light because we are full of both.

The difficulty of owning our shadows is that it requires a lot of vulnerability, something difficult for many of us yet one of the many fruits to come from liminal spaces. If you are not used to your weaknesses and mistakes being met with grace, vulnerability is

---

63. See Ps. 126:5–6.

hard to come by. Believe me, I know. I spent the first half of my life overcompensating for my frailty and weaknesses by masking them with confidence and strength. Only after years of doing inner work have I come to see that it was always the fear of being abandoned that fueled my actions. If I perform well, put on a smiling face, am quick to laugh, and stay in a good mood, others will want to befriend me. As Brené Brown said, "You either walk inside your story and own it or you stand outside your story and hustle for your worthiness."[64] I'm a hustler by nature, manipulating with ease, playing the angles, making sure I come out on top. It's a sinful (and stupid) way to live. It's also very, very tiring for your soul to never know its worth unless it comes in the short bursts of a job well done.

I lived like this not because I despised weakness or vulnerability but because I was scared, insecure, and didn't know how to live otherwise. Of course, by refusing to be honest about our fears and insecurities, we end up producing the very thing we are running from. By not being honest with others about my shortcomings and failures, I wasn't allowing them to know all of me or giving them a chance to love me anyway. Instead, I became a caricature of myself, emphasizing only my strengths and eschewing all the undesirable aspects. That worked out pretty well for longer than it should have—until it didn't. When God led me to the valley of the shadow of death, I feared evil, I feared people, I feared myself. I was no longer able to feign strength and knew I needed to embrace weakness. While I was met with grace from many people who had known me only as competent, in control, and strong, others were not able to extend the same acceptance.

64. Brené Brown, "In You Must Go: Harnessing the Force by Owning Our Stories," *Brené Brown* (blog), May 4, 2018, https://brenebrown.com /blog/2018/05/04/in-you-must-go-harnessing-the-force-by-owning-our -stories/.

One of my mentors likened it to when an alcoholic father becomes sober. He is getting healthy, but no one in the family knows how to relate to him any other way than as an alcoholic.

After a long season of darkness and despair, I began to emerge again with the people I already loved, as well as some new people I was learning to love. When I was given a chance to tell my story for the first time since this period of awakening, I was able to do so by emphasizing my weaknesses and how they led me to live, as well as the strengths I have when I am healthy. This was a way for me to put my weapons on the table, take off the very armor I use to hide, and willingly expose myself to people who could use it to hurt me. That led to a season of great creativity and productivity as I was able to explore all that is true of me, teaching and leading others from that place of reality. Theodore Roosevelt said, "In the long run, the most unpleasant truth is a safer companion than a pleasant falsehood."[65]

The confusing space between death and new life that produces creativity in the arts is the same space that allows us to creatively reimagine our lives. Just as our lives are not static, neither is our understanding of our identity. We are complex creatures, imaging God in a social and relational likeness. If a relationship to others requires an open receptivity to all that they are and are becoming, how much more grace does that require of us? I am not the man I was at 25 or 35 years old, yet certain impulses and desires remain true, finding their expression through age-appropriate means. Discovering our true selves takes a lifetime as we sift through what is changing and evolving and what will always be with us. It is likely truer to say that my understanding of myself at 25 differed from my understanding of myself at 35.

---

65. Theodore Roosevelt, *Theodore Roosevelt's Words of Wit and Wisdom* (New York: Chartwell Books, 2016), 16.

Discovering ourselves requires grace and creativity to allow our souls room to breathe and become the people God is making us to be. It requires letting go of false masks worn by past selves as well as beginning new practices that foster growth and life. I think this is one of the reasons the period we call midlife is so difficult. It requires an honest examination and a reckoning of who we were, are, and would like to become. When we feel like we're only good at being young, that self-examination can be the hardest first step to take. Not only does it require us to recognize that we are getting older, it requires coming to terms with harder truths as well. Our bodies don't work the way they used to, there are some dreams we had for our lives that are never going to happen, and there are very real regrets about our past that are too late to reconcile.

Creative Tension

Let's be honest. Most of us do not even consider changing until we are flat-out stuck. We call it being in a funk, stuck in a rut, or any number of axioms to describe the feeling. When we have tried every available avenue open to us and nothing seems to work, we begin to think outside the box. That is called "creative tension." It is typically used to refer to some kind of circumstance or environment where discord or disagreement gives way to better ideas or outcomes. The felt tension becomes the refiner's fire for our ideas and input. It can come from a clash of ideas in a group context, but it can just as easily come from a liminal situation.

We are already inhabiting the in-between both mentally and physically. We have been living in a place between the old and the new and are primed for something different. That is where true creativity comes from, some kind of tension that the very thing you are prepared to bring into the world does not already exist— the idea, the words, the art, the relationship. Just because it has not already been done does not make that a barrier to attempting it. How God typically fashions His people in these seasons is by giving us a unique mix of skill, personality, and experience, adding pressure to cause something new to emerge and then giving us a divine spark of creativity to mimic His own work in the creation of something new.

Tod Bolsinger tells the story of Lewis and Clark who were tasked with discovering a waterway that would lead all the way to the Pacific Ocean. After they canoed the Missouri River upstream for some time, the terrain changed, and the Rocky Mountains began. These trained paddlers had to adapt from river to mountains, trading their canoes for horses and leading their team to do the same. Bolsinger writes:

> This *adaptive capacity* is the crucial leadership element for a changing world. . . . adaptive capacity is also its own set of skills to be mastered. These skills include the capacity to
>
> - calmly face the unknown
> - refuse quick fixes
> - engage others in the learning and transformation necessary to take on the challenge that is before them
> - seek new perspectives
> - ask questions that reveal competing values and gaps in values and actions
> - raise up the deeper issues at work in a community[66]

---

66. Tod Bolsinger, *Canoeing the Mountains* (Westmont, IL: IVP Books, 2018), 90.

Adaptive capacity and creative tension are the catalyst for the kind of creativity required to chart a new way forward when we are stuck. Rather than "canoeing the mountains," we are forced to think through the same problem in a different way, learn to sit with the change desired and the roadblocks to accomplishing it, and trust God during the long, slow process.

In 2020 during the COVID-19 pandemic, everything shut down seemingly overnight. We went from living a normal, maybe even boring life to having everything turn upside down with such rapidity that it took a while to fully process all we lost after the initial lockdowns. My work of engaging and training churches to better serve vulnerable children in the foster care system shut down immediately. For the first several months of the pandemic, churches turned their attention inward, focusing on their own congregations and how to care for them. Many churches learned how to livestream for the first time ever, and online church became a household phrase for most Christians, even those (like me) who previously would have hated the idea. After some time, churches began to lift their eyes up and turn their attention outward as they realized that not everyone was "safer at home."

During this period, calls to the child abuse hotline went down 50 percent. That had nothing to do with less abuse or neglect (there was more) but from having fewer eyes looking into the lives of these children. There was no in-person interaction from teachers, nurses, or coaches interacting with children whose only outlet away from the nightmare of their home lives was school or sports. Suddenly trapped in the same house with struggling parents, many who lost their jobs at the time, led to a greater danger for these kids. The opportunity for churches to meaningfully engage their communities was never higher. Some took advantage of it, even hiring new staff to lead the way in caring for at-risk children and families. Others talked about getting around to it "when things went back to normal." For all the talk of this being our "new normal," there was very little normalcy in our lives, and for the better part of a year, things changed week by week as we learned how widespread this disease had become.

The catalyst for some churches to find new and creative ways to embody the good news of Jesus also proved to be the stated reason why other churches doubled down on getting back to the way things used to be. Without anyone to cast a vision for the future, to lead through adaptive capacity and creative tension, they just got stuck. For those who have been talking about decentralizing the hierarchy of the traditional Western church, this was a gift. In two weeks, God accomplished more than what we had been pushing for decades to happen. For those committed to the status quo, this proved to be a challenge they were unable to overcome. Many churches shut down during this time, some from overburdened pastors unable to continue, some from congregations freshly divided over social ills, and others from financial troubles. Some churches tried to replicate the in-person worship experience by becoming professionals at lighting, staging, and livestreaming their music and sermons. Very few asked themselves what the purpose of Sunday mornings actually was. Instead, they settled for trying to reproduce an online version of what they had done for so long in person. I can tell you that during this time, I was not at a loss for good teaching. I did not miss sitting in a seat in a building to hear the exposition of God's Word. I had podcasts, webinars, video calls, and any number of means to continue to hear from both local and national teachers. I created new worship playlists on Spotify and immersed myself in them when I needed to pause and remember God. I was lacking for none of these things, yet these things were what some churches were scrambling to reproduce.

As pastors, we couldn't turn to anyone and ask what they'd done during the last global pandemic. There was no contemporary wisdom or playbook for what to do during such a time as this. There was only the creative tension of discovering new ways to embody the ancient truths of Scripture.

Some churches began working in a new, creative, liminal space, reimagining ways to connect people to each other, to share their stories, to bring the truth of God's Word into our homes, our families, our workplaces. They found entirely new ways to serve their communities, some through means they would never have encountered unless they were forced to reevaluate. I had a front-row seat to watch both happen and came out of it with an ever greater appreciation for how difficult it is to lead into the unknown when there is no one who has done it before. Instead of canoeing the mountains, we had to adapt to new terrain and new challenges by using new tools and solutions. The only thing that stayed the same was the fierce love and concern God has for His people and the same Spirit that once led the church to explore new ways of following Jesus in Acts 2, empowering us to do the same.

Φ

CHAPTER SIX: NEW CREATIONS TAKE TIME

Abide in me, and I in you. As the branch cannot bear fruit by itself, unless it abides in the vine, neither can you, unless you abide in me. I am the vine; you are the branches.

—John 15:4–5

I want to break these bones 'til they're better
I want to break them right and feel alive
You were wrong, you were wrong, you were wrong—
My healing needed more than time.

—Sleeping at Last, "Eight"

What Time Is It?

The Bible primarily uses two words—*chronos* and *kairos*—to describe time as humanity's place in a temporal world as it moves forward through eternity. Personified as gods in Greek literature, *chronos* symbolizes the forward march of time, while *kairos* refers to the perfect time for something.

One of the most disturbing paintings I've seen is of the Greek god Chronos by painter Francisco Goya. As the story goes, Chronos (also Cronus or Saturn) learns of a prophecy that his son will replace him as he replaced his father. Taking matters into his own hands, he decides to eat his children. This story is a graphic depiction of the way temporal time works, devouring what came before to make way for what is to be. We are all familiar with chronological time—minutes to hours, hours to days, days to weeks, weeks to months, months to years. Tireless and unrelenting, time marches on without our input or permission. Chronos time is constantly moving. We can't slow it down or stop it, and once it's lost, we can't get it back. Kairos time requires the kind of creativity and abstract thinking discussed in the last chapter. When we ask, "What time is it?" the answer is best expressed in chronological terms. If we ask, "What is this time for?" we get closer to the heart of kairos, which means an appointed time, a ripe season, or an opportune moment. In Galatians, it is used to describe the birth of Christ. "But when the fullness of time [*kairos*] had come, God sent forth his Son, born of woman, born under the law" (Gal. 4:4). Chronos devours, but kairos enlarges. Chronos drives us with its insistent ticking, but kairos expands the possibilities of what God is doing in a given moment. It is the language of discipleship, of redeeming the time.[67] Kairos means we are awake, aware, and

---

67. See Eph. 5:16.

alert, keeping an eye out for what is happening around us and acting when the moment is right. It teaches us that some moments are more important than others, when the time is just right for God to awaken us to an opportunity.

Is there a better expression of kairos time in our lives than when we are forced to wait on God? While chronos can make waiting feel like a prison, kairos is a multipurpose tool in the hands of God. Time can wear down channels and grooves, like the Colorado River running through the Grand Canyon. Time can age, time can make bitter, time can heal, but ultimately, time will kill. Consider it one ingredient in the mix, the activating agent for what or, more specifically, *who* does the actual healing.

One of the difficulties with waiting is that it often comes to us unbidden. We haven't asked for it, and we don't find it particularly helpful. It is an unwanted guest who comes without invitation, eats all our food, drinks all our wine, and stays too long. Yet in this forced liminality, we are pressed to confront deeper issues that have been under the surface for a long time. We struggle with a layoff that reveals how much of our identity was tied up in what we do. Our bodies age and decay, and we are no longer able to do the things that previously brought us joy. The dreams we had for ourselves have slipped away and have not been replaced. We are disappointed in God, others, and ourselves. It exposes how much we struggle living in the midst of a broken world, left to make sense of this already but not yet Kingdom of God. This is what makes it kairos time. It comes to us circumstantially and is meant to serve as a mirror, among other things.

It is when we look to Christ as our teacher that we learn the pain of waiting is the classroom where Jesus actually does His work of redemption. There is something about the human soul that requires these difficulties to grow into maturity. Rather than a sign that God has removed His favor from us, leaving us to wait, wonder, and pray for difficulties to end, we can see this time as the path God has marked out for us to be transformed into the image of Christ. When we seek to avoid suffering, placating ourselves with a life of one exciting event to the next, we sabotage the maturation process—the very reason for the waiting in the first place. Like a skilled surgeon, Jesus at times does use a scalpel, but only to cut out the cancer that will ultimately destroy us.

I recently moved into a home advertised as "great for entertaining." Indeed, it would one day be great for entertaining once we had windows that closed, a functioning kitchen, and seating for our large family. We moved in with the bravado that comes from actually "owning-ish" a home—high hopes that we would make it ours. But as we played the ultimate game of Tetris in the moving truck with all our belongings, we realized that unloading the truck would be impossible until we had some work done on the house. For a family of six who had rented our entire lives, we were used to living as is and making do with what we could afford in the meantime, usually some new accessories and switch plates from the hardware store. But between the period of moving by faith and the work of renovation, we were stuck until others more competent than I am fixed what was broken. It was the proverbial carrot on a stick, moving forward with project after project yet never feeling truly able to relax. Each weekend brought a fresh slate of projects, from small ones like patching some drywall to larger ones like waiting for the popcorn ceiling throughout the house to be scraped, sanded, primed, and painted. We were buoyed along by the hope of how good it would look when it was finally done, which made it easier to stomach not having an oven or a stove that worked. Even when the annual fires broke out in Southern California and fresh deposits of ash were left on the inside windowsills and floors from old crank windows that wouldn't close, we were hopeful. There was a future reality we were working toward that made the in-between a little more bearable.

This is not unlike the reality of waiting on the Lord for the renovation of our earthly temples—body, soul, and mind being transformed from glory to glory.[68] In fact, James, the half brother of Jesus, puts it this way in his book: "Dear brothers and sisters, when troubles of any kind come your way, consider it an opportunity for great joy. For you know that when your faith is tested, your endurance has a chance to grow. So let it grow, for when your endurance is fully developed, you will be perfect and complete, needing nothing" (James 1:2–4 NLT). He encourages us so we can know the testing of our faith (unseen things hoped for with assurance) will produce patience. And patience fosters the work of maturity, and in that we will lack nothing. Notice that he doesn't say the fulfillment of our testing (maturity) provides all we have need of, but the experience of the testing with the needed patience and endurance during the in-between.

Paul says something similar in his letter to the church at Rome. "Through him [Jesus Christ] we have also obtained access by faith into this grace in which we stand, and we rejoice in hope of the glory of God. Not only that, but we rejoice in our sufferings, knowing that suffering produces endurance, and endurance produces character, and character produces hope" (Rom. 5:2–4). The similarities of these two men's writings are striking—we "count it all joy" and "rejoice in our sufferings" *knowing that* these trials and tribulations produce patience and endurance, which then produces character and maturity, which in turn produces hope.

---

68. See 2 Cor. 3:18.

There is nothing distinctly Christian in these truths. The rain falls on the just and unjust alike, and seasons of suffering are the fate of all humanity. In his memorable poem, "Along the Road," Robert Browning Hamilton writes:

> I walked a mile with Pleasure;
> She chattered all the way,
> But left me none the wiser
> For all she had to say.
>
> I walked a mile with Sorrow
> And ne'er a word said she;
> But oh, the things I learned from her
> When Sorrow walked with me![69]

What is distinctly Christian is our ability to now embrace suffering because of the life, death, and resurrection of Jesus. The prophet Isaiah tells us, "It was our weaknesses he carried; it was our sorrows that weighed him down. . . . He was beaten so we could be whole. He was whipped so we could be healed" (Isa. 53:4–5 NLT).

It would appear that God has orchestrated the redemptive process to include hardship, affliction, various external trials, and mixed internal temptations. This is the path He has marked out for all who desire to be transformed into the image of Christ. To repeat, there is something about the human soul that requires difficulties to reach maturity.

The overlap of the previous passages from James and Romans is that it is assumed, not explicitly mentioned, that it takes

---

69. Robert Browning Hamilton, "Along the Road," Poetry Nook, accessed June 22, 2021, https://www.poetrynook.com/poem/along-road.

a lot of time for patience and endurance to have their perfect work in our lives. And that is where the vulnerability, weakness, and hard work begin. As a new Christian, I was struck by the imagery of being a new creation that the Apostle Paul described. "Therefore, if anyone is in Christ, he is a new creation. The old has passed away; behold, the new has come" (2 Cor. 5:17). That sounded like a wonderful promise of immediate change, which in part was true. When I turned my life over to Jesus, a lot changed almost from day one. I stopped medicating myself with drugs, alcohol, and sex. I found a great church and became part of a loving community, and I began spending time in fruitful and life-giving ways. Sure, it took me another year to finally quit smoking cigarettes, but even that was easier knowing that Jesus had redeemed my life for a greater purpose. Paul goes on to say:

> But as servants of God we commend ourselves in every way: by great endurance, in afflictions, hardships, calamities, beatings, imprisonments, riots, labors, sleepless nights, hunger; by purity, knowledge, patience, kindness, the Holy Spirit, genuine love; by truthful speech, and the power of God; with the weapons of righteousness for the right hand and for the left; through honor and dishonor, through slander and praise. We are treated as impostors, and yet are true; as unknown, and yet well known; as dying, and behold, we live; as punished, and yet not killed; as sorrowful, yet always rejoicing; as poor, yet making many rich; as having nothing, yet possessing everything.
>
> —2 Cor. 6:4–10

Nothing about this passage sounds immediate or as if Jesus magically takes all hardships away from the start. Looking back, I think I interpreted many of the passages about hardships as referring to external difficulties we were meant to endure and overcome. I met many of these trials with faith in the living God and hope for a better future. What I didn't expect to find was that my internal battles would be the biggest obstacle to my own growth in Christ-likeness. As the old cartoon character Pogo said, "We have met the enemy, and he is us."[70] I did not yet realize that I had developed extremely complex internal ways of assuming my own innocence as a means of self-protection until much later. There are some demons that are not cast out without dark, sleepless nights, knowing that we are imposters yet somehow authentic; unseen, yet well-known; poor while making many rich; having nothing while possessing everything.[71] All of this was grace that came to me during several dark nights of the soul. I, like many of us, found it easier to pin the cause of all my suffering on external forces, unwanted distractions from the upward call of God in Christ Jesus.[72]

Extended seasons of waiting on God force us to look inward and see how we are the common denominator of every difficulty in our lives. For me, every layer of my own culpability led me to unearth why I was so committed to self-deception. What was it I was trying to protect by not admitting my own shadow side of sinfulness? If our actions are the tip of the iceberg of our hearts, then we need deep inner work to become completely honest with

70. "We Have Met the Enemy and He Is Us," Billy Ireland Cartoon Library & Museum, accessed June 22, 2021, https://library.osu.edu/site/40stories/2020/01/05/we-have-met-the-enemy/.
71. See 2 Cor. 6:8–10.
72. See Phil. 3:14.

ourselves about what we are protecting. During long seasons of waiting, through a loving community of family and friends who asked good questions and were not afraid of less-than-noble answers, I discovered a layer to my story I never knew existed. By telling my story honestly, allowing for piercing questions and observations by those around me (especially my insightful wife), I uncovered a through line of being abandoned and confused throughout my life. Being left by friends and loved ones has marked my life since childhood without any clear reason why. In the absence of answers, I filled in the gaps of my own broken narrative by assuming I am not good enough, lovable enough, or worth staying by when I am not performing at peak capacity. That belief led me to overfunction for myself and others in order to prove my own sense of worth. They were deep waters only to be waded through with time, intentional counseling, and gut-wrenching honesty.

For someone like me, it is easier to work through that pain by keeping busy, performing well, and receiving a modicum of affirmation for a job well done. The only problem is that at some point, the curtain closes, the audience files out, and the applause dies down. Being content in the quiet place alone requires more than getting what we think we deserve. That is why waiting is what leaves us in that raw place of openness, the same waiting we are tempted to move past all too quickly in order to get back to the real work of glorifying God. Then we are forced to consider this: What if the work of waiting is the greatest way we are glorifying God at this moment? What if the questions themselves, not the answers, are glorifying God in our lives in a way that nothing else can? Is it possible that the longing for wholeness is just as satisfying to God as our faltering, fumbling pursuit of it?

God is jealous for our affections, and He will take all the time in the world, which for Him is as a day,[73] to purify our loves and desires until they are fixed entirely on Him. Removing the immediate affirmations that we grow accustomed to is a severe mercy for our souls to return to our first love, to repent and do the works we did at first.[74]

A Time for Suffering

> *But it was the LORD's good plan to crush him and cause him grief.*
>
> —Isa. 53:10 NLT

That is such a jarring sentence, offensive to our modern sensibilities and certainly unwelcome in a Christian culture of triumphalism. Yet here we have Isaiah's well-known prophecy of the Christ who would suffer for our sorrows, weaknesses, and sins. What if it's true? We know the right answer, but what if God's plan A was not only to cause Jesus grief but also to completely crush him like the grapes of harvest that the fruit of the vine might bring joy to others? What would that mean for those who patiently waited with Jesus during the in-between? I believe there are three truths that can guide our painful waiting under the tutelage of the Master Teacher.

First, suffering with Jesus provides us an opportunity to become more like God. This is a common enough statement, usually received gladly when the means of knowing Him is through His resurrection power. But when given the invitation to know Him

---

73. See Ps. 90:4, 2 Pet. 3:8.
74. See Rev. 2:5.

through the fellowship of suffering,[75] we struggle with seeing the value. Admittedly, it seems like a hard trade-off, my present happiness and contentment for the future possibility of knowing Jesus better. But this view reveals how little we think of the actual reality that we might not only become a student and lover of Jesus but also experience more of His presence through suffering. A patient disciple knows that only by following Jesus into the pain and sorrow can we, too, deem the Lord's plan good, not in spite of but because of the actual suffering. And by experiencing the disconcerting feeling of liminality—the disappointment, despair, and hopelessness—we can learn to loosen our grip on all else we cling to for meaning and purpose. Our jobs, spouses, children, friendships, and churches can finally find their proper place, not as the source of our happiness but as the recipients of our life in Christ.

Second, suffering with Jesus creates true empathy and witness to a world without hope. This is what Paul is getting at with his cryptic statement about "filling up what is lacking in Christ's afflictions for the sake of his body" (Col. 1:24). When we personally experience a taste of Christ's afflictions, we are participating in the drama of redemption on behalf of others. Paul sees his suffering as a visible reenactment of the sufferings of Christ so others may see Christ's love for them. Every time we choose to walk the lesser traveled road of suffering, we are making a statement with our lives about the deep love of Christ that can never be taken from us. The prophet Isaiah reminds us that we, too, once "thought his troubles were a punishment from God, a punishment for his own sins" (Isa. 53:4 NLT) but learned that as He was "pierced for our rebellion, crushed for our sins" (Isa. 53:5 NLT), we are made whole and healed through His suffering. Our difficulties do not

---

75. See Phil. 3:10.

mean God has abandoned us or left us to figure out life on our own. They are not a reminder of past sin or prior mistakes. They are a reality of life in a fallen world, yet another tragedy that Jesus came to redeem.

I once had a conversation with a young girl in our church who had just had a miscarriage. She and her husband already had one child and were looking to grow their family. She asked me why God would allow her to lose a child while other less fit parents continued to have children. Before I could speak, she answered her own question. "Pastor, I just know that God is punishing me." When I inquired why she thought that, she began listing all the things she had done that were outside of God's desires for her. While my heart broke for the grief and loss she was experiencing, my mind was stuck thinking about how bad theology was plaguing her. She was confusing an invitation to experience Jesus's afflictions as a witness to others (among other things) with the thought that God was making her an example of what happens when you disobey God.

Of course, "filling up what is lacking" is not referring to the sacrifice of Jesus being anything less than perfect and complete. There can be no punishment for our past sins if they were all laid on Jesus who experienced the bitterest death so we could be free. There is no reason for God to punish us when Jesus has taken away the reason for punishment and when there is no wrath left in His cup of judgment. Instead, we can walk with Jesus in the painful afflictions and trials, knowing that rather than being punished for sins long ago, we are instead shouting to a dying world the reality of the unchanging love of God through the sacrifice of Jesus. While it doesn't grant immunity from any future trials, the goodness of God remains in our darkest times of waiting, and there has never been a saint who saw otherwise in hindsight.

Third, suffering allows us to get a glimpse of just how dark and wicked the sin that sent Jesus to the cross was, which in turn allows us to get a glimpse of how truly thankful we should be. I find there are seasons in my life when sin becomes more of an abstract concept and less of a concrete example of the darkness in my own heart. I'm sitting down writing this on Good Friday, meditating on the cross. My heart needs the reminder that it wasn't just the love of God for me that led Jesus to be pierced, but it was also his hatred of the sin that leads me away from Him by so easily ensnaring and entangling my heart.[76] As much as we do violence to our sin and crucify it daily, part of our humanity means living in a broken world with broken bodies and broken desires. Despite our best intentions and sincerity, there is always a personal propensity toward something destructive.

To value the cross of Jesus more highly, I must recognize the inherent vice in myself more readily. For my misguided thoughts, words, and actions, He was pierced. For my misguided desires, He was crushed. For my misguided love of control, power, safety, and comfort, He was crucified. And when Jesus accomplished His greatest miracle of all, making His life an offering for sin, He was satisfied. "When he sees all that is accomplished by his anguish, he will be satisfied, and because of his experience, my righteous servant will make it possible for many to be counted righteous, for he will bear all their sins" (Isa. 53:11 NLT). This verse is talking about me. Despite my sin, I am the one who was made righteous through His death, and I know of nothing else but the truth that restores the joy of my salvation. Rather than producing guilt or despair, the recognition of sin leads to gratefulness and thanksgiving.

---

76. See Heb. 12:1.

How does this look practically? We must begin to take a view of time that is in line with God's. Peter, the impetuous, hot-tempered disciple, encourages us in his mature years: "Do not overlook this one fact, beloved, that with the Lord one day is as a thousand years, and a thousand years as one day. The Lord is not slow to fulfill his promise as some count slowness, but is patient toward you, not wishing that any should perish, but that all should reach repentance" (2 Pet. 3:8–9). The Lord, who is patient, desires His beloved to be honestly led to repentance, not self-justification. The journey from self-justification to honest acceptance takes more time than we would like. His patience is the progenitor of ours and necessitates more time than we may be comfortable with. Patience, by definition, is our capacity to tolerate delay without getting angry. The Bible insists that learning this lesson will lead to our maturity—an advanced stage of our emotional, mental, and spiritual development. And that is good news!

A Time for Endings and New Beginnings

As time plays itself out in seasons of speed and interminable leisure, we are introduced to the way God moves in our lives. When life seems to be moving along according to plan, we can become lulled into the sleep of the comfortable. When life throws us into a tailspin, we develop a heightened awareness of our lack of control. Both sensations are from the same God who views time much differently than we do. In his commentary on Ecclesiastes, pastor and author Zack Eswine says, "God intends you to know him by requiring you to look plainly and without polish at yourself, your neighbors, and the world in which you and I live."[77]

---

77. Zack Eswine, *Recovering Eden: The Gospel According to Ecclesiastes* (Phillipsburg, NJ: P & R Publishing, 2014), 3.

One of the times we come face-to-face with ourselves and others is during these in-between spaces of waiting. These are times when the Spirit of God causes us to honestly view God, ourselves, and others in order to redirect our paths. If becoming a new creation takes time, we can expect part of that time to require death as well as resurrection. We are forced to confront when we have come to an end of our abilities and are wading in the waters of limitations. These limitations, however, are also gifts meant to remind us that only One is perfect and always does what is right. As we become more aware of both our abilities and limitations, we become more like Jesus who, without argument, seemed to know exactly what the Father had asked Him to be and do and what He had not.

Psalm 31:24 tells us, "Be strong, and let your heart take courage, all you who wait for the LORD!" The fact that we need to be reminded so often to be strong, take courage, wait in patience, and trust in the Lord shows us how hard it actually is to wait. It requires strength to lean on the Lord in our weakness, and it requires courage to continue to move forward despite the frustration in the barrenness and the unknown.

That is where endings and new beginnings come into play. In order for anything new to grow, death is required. Jesus taught His disciples that unless a grain of wheat falls to the ground and dies, it remains alone; but if it dies, it bears much fruit.[78] This paradox is central to our understanding of Scripture and how we align our lives with the Bible. We struggle to understand how life can come from death, but not only is that true in the Bible, it is also true in every area of life. Some time ago, my family was on vacation in Sequoia National Park, one of our favorite places to go. I overheard a park ranger mention the term *prescribed burn*,

---

78. See John 12:24.

which I had never heard before. Apparently, the ecology there needs fire for survival since it clears existing brush, fertilizes the ground, and leaves good soil for things to grow. Those massive, ancient redwoods have trouble reproducing without some burning around them, and controlled burns are one of the best tools to prevent uncontrolled fires.

It is amazing how God can use the fire from a season of death to clear the soil for a season of new life, reproduction, and fruit-bearing. Instead of getting stuck in the past, we follow Jesus into death and walk through it into resurrection. Death and endings are as natural as birth and life, but they carry the stigma of failure and shame rather than optimism and success. Pete Scazzero, author of *Emotionally Healthy Spirituality*, writes and speaks about this idea quite a bit. His premise is that most of us don't do well with endings, and as a result we miss many new beginnings God has for us. He gives these specific examples of how you can determine if you're not dealing with endings well:

- You can't stop ruminating about something from the past.
- You use busyness as an excuse to avoid taking time to grieve endings and losses.
- You have a hard time identifying your difficult feelings (sadness, fear, anger).
- You often find yourself angry and frustrated by the limits and pain of life.
- You escape or medicate the pain of loss through keeping busy or self-destructive behaviors such as overeating, inappropriate relationships, overengagement with social media, or working too much.
- You struggle with envy toward those who don't seem to struggle with the same struggles and hardship in life you do.

- You often dream of quitting in order to avoid the disappointments and setbacks that routinely characterize leadership.
- You are not honest with yourself about your feelings, doubts, and hurts.
- You rarely acknowledge directly that a program or person has outright failed.
- You avoid pain by spinning the truth and glossing over leadership losses and disappointments.[79]

That's a pretty good list of indicators to help us see whether we need to grow in this area. Ecclesiastes is clear: there is a time to give up and move on.[80] Wisdom requires us to know when that time is. What in your life needs to die? Is there something God might be asking you to open your hands and let go of in order to bring about something new? Here are some examples.

In the churches I have pastored, there have been some existing ministries that should have ended years ago, but a long-time member of the church couldn't see that it no longer accomplished what it once did. It may have been a ministry that was incredibly effective 20 years ago but no longer has the same effect in the cultural landscape. The same is true of any program at work that someone feels passionate about but is no longer in line with the goals of the staff or organization.

You may find an employee you hired who used to be a good fit on the team but has stopped performing or whose position is no longer needed for the direction of the staff. To free up the budget

---

79. Pete Scazzero, "Endings and New Beginnings in Leadership," Emotionally Healthy Discipleship, February 11, 2015, https://www.emotionally healthy.org/endings-and-new-beginnings-in-leadership/.
80. See Eccles. 4:1–8.

to hire someone better for the organization, you have to make a hard decision.

There might be a toxic relationship in your life that requires a different set of boundaries than you have in place. You may feel guilty about ending the relationship or friendship because you think Christians are supposed to love indiscriminately and reconcile when there is any disagreement whatsoever.

You might have an ingrained way of spending your time that needs to die such as mindless scrolling through social media, procrastination, ways of leading meetings, not planning ahead for future ideas, and the list goes on. Sometimes we have moments of clarity when we can see that more effort in the same direction is not likely to bring about a different result.

Whatever it is, if we normalize, accept, and even embrace an ending, we can better understand that everything has a set life cycle.

A Time for Unfinished Business

"Maturity is the ability to tolerate the incompleteness of life." A mentor shared that with me some years ago, and it rings true every day of my life. Maturity is being able to live in the liminal, in-between spaces of pain and uncertainty long after innocence is lost and long before solutions are found. Most of life is actually lived there, and our maturity is directly related to our pain tolerance threshold. I have spent most of my life trying to avoid pain and have well-worn habits that make it easier to live detached and distant rather than open and present. It takes a lot more effort for me to intentionally live by a different value than safety and self-protection.

When we decided to open our home to children in need of one, we knew it would be hard and were prepared for that. We knew life would become messy and chaotic, and we were prepared for that as well. What we weren't prepared for was the toll that receiving four children under the age of eight would take on our existing family of six. In a choice typical for us, our family went big and wanted desperately to keep a set of four siblings together after they were removed from their mother. In the end, we were unable to do so without doing severe damage to our marriage, our biological children, and our family system. We decided to keep the youngest of the four and find another family to take the other three. I wrestled with anticipating how the kids would make sense of this chapter of their lives. Events as painful as this have a way of searing into our memories until they become part of the script of our lives. What would theirs be, that the people who said they loved them would leave them? Am I too difficult to love? Do I need to behave a certain way to be worthy of love?

I don't know how the children will internalize their story as they get older, but thinking about my inability to save them and welcome them into my family forever generates an incredible amount of shame, anxiety, and pain inside me. In another twist I couldn't have anticipated, their abandonment now hits very close to home to some of my life scripts and wounds from a young age. Due to these forces, I've become embroiled in what Brené Brown calls a "shame shitstorm."[81] There are two competing stories, both true and both full of pain. Neither will be resolved quickly or without a lot of work. Maturity requires that I show up in the midst of this painful messiness with questions that have no answers, negative feelings that have no resolution, and the reality that I have taken responsibility to fix a problem I did not create. I willingly chose to step into someone else's bad decisions and alleviate the

---

81. *Brené Brown: The Call to Courage*, directed by Sandra Restrepo, Los Angeles: Netflix, 2019.

brunt of the pain inflicted on children who had no fault other than being born. I also willingly chose to acknowledge my own deep sense of shame, feeling of inadequacy, and unpreparedness for old wounds to hurt me again. This is the storm of thoughts, emotions, and old narratives we can get swept up in, leaving us feeling dazed and confused.

Serving children in the foster care system, in whatever capacity, is the greatest tool I've found to build up a tolerance for pain. Even the smoothest transition still requires a child to be removed from their parents, their home, and their community, with all the trauma that goes along with it. Like Westley's immunity to iocane powder in *The Princess Bride*, we spend years developing a tolerance. One incident, tantrum, and outburst after another develop our tolerance to hear and hold painful stories, wanting someone to blame but finding no easy target, or finding a target that is too easy. Sometimes it feels like we must find an outlet for all our sadness and anger lest they spill out on others equally unresponsible for our outburst. This is the ministry of caring for orphans. This is how we enter their story, signing up to hold them while they are trying to scream at the nearest adult, committing to a patient perseverance with them as they act out of trauma they did not cause.

As our tolerance for pain grows, our ability to thrive in the liminal spaces also grows exponentially. What freedom it is to live in this place of unresolved hurts without hurting others! It is moving in a place of sadness and trauma without feeling responsible to fix, change, or control it. It is listening to stories of the most gut-wrenching degradation and not withdraw in fear because we have no answers and are afraid of saying the wrong thing. Just keep showing up day by day as Jesus does His slow work of redemption—in them and in us.

CHAPTER SIX

In her wonderful essay about our inner lives, philosopher
Martha Nussbaum says this:

*And even though we develop a degree of mastery and
independence, we always remain alarmingly weak and
incomplete, dependent on others and on an uncertain
world for whatever we are able to achieve. . . . Our
emotional life maps our incompleteness: A creature
without any needs would never have reasons for fear,
or grief, or hope, or anger. But for that very reason we
are often ashamed of our emotions, and of the relations
of need and dependency bound up with them.*[82]

It is precisely this incompleteness that puts our humanity on
display and provides the kinds of lessons that produce maturity.
We never arrive. We never get there, wherever we think that might
be. Like the Colorado River slowly carving out the Grand Canyon
over time or the way rough edges of stone become smoother in
the path of that same river, we, too, may experience a bettering of
our lives and still remain incomplete. Our well-being was never
contingent on strength, success, or stability. So we lean into the
moments we feel weak, unprepared, exposed, off-balance, and
unsure, knowing loose ends and half-tied knots don't always
mean something negative.

Father Richard Rohr calls this the spirituality of imperfection. Ironically, we experience greater spiritual growth by doing
things wrong rather than doing them right. Spiritual maturity
seems to emerge precisely from how we handle the imperfections

---

82. *Take My Advice: Letters to the Next Generation from People Who Know
a Thing or Two,* ed. James L. Harmon (New York: Simon & Shuster, 2007).

all around us, especially in ourselves. A "perfect" person ends up being one who can consciously allow, forgive, and embrace imperfection in themselves and others. Those unable to do so opt for perfectionism, a bastardization of the biblical concept of being perfect as our Father in heaven is perfect.[83] Perfectionism does not lead to honest self-knowledge, much less the ability to even desire such. It also does not produce the humility necessary to be able to pursue Jesus in Spirit and in truth.[84] In her book *The Gifts of Imperfection*, Brené Brown writes:

> *Perfectionism is not the same thing as striving to be your best. Perfectionism is the belief that if we live perfect, look perfect, and act perfect, we can minimize or avoid the pain of blame, judgement [sic], and shame. It's a shield. It's a twenty-ton shield that we lug around thinking it will protect us when, in fact, it's the thing that's really preventing us from flight.*[85]

Perfectionism can come from an environment where failure is not allowed—by parents, teachers, coaches, or even ourselves. Whatever the source, it is a cheap imitation of being truly good with a purity of intention and action. It can manufacture only a cold, judgmental attitude that is quick to speak, slow to listen, and slowest to admit fault. Without a gospel big enough to carry all our insufficiencies, we are left to rely on our own judgments and justification for the forgiveness of sin. Jesus's offer of unconditional love based on accepting His perfection sounds like an offer to which I could more freely surrender my imperfections.

---

83. See Matt. 5:48.
84. See John 4:23.
85. Brené Brown, *The Gifts of Imperfection* (New York: Random House, 2010).

Pursuing this kind of maturity truly is the best way to redeem the time. If kairos time is an expansive opportunity to wait with Jesus in between the ending of one thing and the beginning of another, why would we reject His invitation? In the face of confusion and disorientation, we are secure with the Lord as our portion and our cup of blessing. He guards all that is important to us, reminding us that the boundary lines have fallen to us in pleasant places and that we have a beautiful inheritance.[86] If new creations take time, then spending time by focusing on these truths sounds like an incredible way to wait on God to work out His purposes in our lives.

---

86. See Ps. 16:5–6.

CO
CO
ON

Pain.
My body is consuming itself, eating and destroying
Everything that I used to be
I look at myself and see what once was
Morphing into new parts
Ugly, untried, unused.
How can this be fitting for a Queen?
How can this pain be freeing?
How long will the tenderness last?
How long until the next name is given to me?
Selfishly I wonder: Will children still look at me with adoring eyes?
How will these new parts help me crawl longer, faster, stronger?
Will I be looked on with horror and fear?
Will I be able to handle their scorn?
This time, there are no reassuring voices,
No encouragement, no affirmation
Just the dull throbbing sound of voices outside
That sound as distant and numb as I feel
Inside is full of darkness and pain
So I created the hard shell around me.
My silk, once fine as thread
Now hardens, repels, and protects me
At the point of complete despair and confusion
the most helpful parts of me fall away
No longer mouth to chew, but tongue for sipping
Nor legs, but crumpled, wet, appendages hanging limply at my side
Fearing the familiar hunger will return with no ability to satiate
I sink deeper into this pit of never-ending night.

Φ

CHAPTER SEVEN:
MAKING TIME TO CREATE
THE FUTURE: PLANNED
LIMINALITY

Fly idleness, which yet thou canst not fly
By dressing, dating, and compliment.
If those take up thy day, the sun will cry
Against thee: for his light was only lent.
                    —George Herbert, *The Temple*

One of the tasks for those who follow Jesus into the unknown is to understand that waiting on God is not something done to us (passive acceptance) but something we actually have agency in (intentional pursuit). To be sure, there are seasons in our lives when waiting is the only option we have due to circumstances, limitations, or other external factors. Yet the command to wait on the Lord is not a military order to be done under threat of punishment but an invitation to use the open space in our lives to actively pursue God.

One of my mentors distinguished between clean pain and dirty pain. Clean pain is felt when we know it is God Himself standing with a flaming sword in our way, and our only responsibility is to seek God and take responsibility for getting closer to Jesus. Dirty pain comes in the form of consequences for our unwise actions, and our responsibility is to work through how we got there in the first place. In both situations, the pain is real and must be acknowledged as real. The difference is that clean pain comes as an invitation to pursue Jesus, while dirty pain comes as an invitation to repent, have our minds renewed, and reengage in healthier ways. I want to suggest a third way to create the same tension and motivation to change as pain does, which I call planned liminality.

This invitation comes to us when things are typically going well-ish. We feel no noticeable pain but also no noticeable joys. Trapped in the mundane, we have no highs or lows to focus on. For me, that experience came after hitting what authors Janet Hagberg and Robert Guelich call "the Wall" in their excellent book *The Critical Journey*.[87] Using imagery from St. John of the Cross's phrase "the dark night of the soul," the authors describe the period in life when we feel stuck between who we have been for the last season of our life and who we want to become in a future season. While it is typically the most painful of the stages of the critical journey, it is also the stage bathed the most in grace, goodness, and the mercy that follows us even in the valley of the shadow of death. As we walk through the valley, David tells us

---

87. Janet O. Hagberg and Robert A. Guelich, *The Critical Journey, Stages in the Life of Faith* (Salem, WI: Sheffield Publishing, 2004), 115.

in the Bible that we do not need to fear any evil, for God's rod and staff (His strength and guidance) comfort us.[88] He prepares a banquet table for us that is filled with all kinds of food and drink, and we get to evaluate what we desire to eat and what we don't.

The period known as the Wall is, above all else, a time of self-evaluation, self-reflection, and deep self-awareness of what is at play in our souls. We typically need to take stock of regret we hold and make a host of decisions about the kind of life we desire to live, especially if that has never been our practice in the past. In their explanation of this stage in our spiritual lives, Hagberg and Guelich describe the Wall as a place of inner choices when things just aren't working anymore and we begin to desire more from life. Going through the Wall requires discomfort, surrender, healing, awareness, forgiveness, risk, acceptance, love, closeness to God, discernment, solitude, and reflection.[89] God Himself will lead us to seasons of planned liminality for any number of reasons. If we have matured to the point where listening to His voice is our only lifeline, then we are ready to actively listen to His voice first rather than letting God orchestrate different circumstances than the one we are in. Here are four keys to using this time in a productive way that develops us as beloved sons and daughters of God.

1. A Season of Waiting

If there are no major life decisions we need to make at this point, we can choose to enter a season of waiting. Rather than seeing this as something negative being done to keep us from the real task of building our lives externally, we can joyfully submit to the season of hiddenness, knowing the work that Jesus wants to do

---

88. See Ps. 23:4.
89. Hagberg and Guelich, *The Critical Journey*, 120.

lies deep under the surface. Any true, deep soul work necessitates a lengthy amount of time. Waiting breaks us out of our cultural captivity to the almighty clock that drives us to relentlessly perform, produce, and proliferate. In Psalm 90, Moses also tells us that a thousand years in God's sight are but as yesterday when it is past, or as a watch in the night.[90] He then goes on to ask God as a result, "Teach *us* to number our days, that we may gain a heart of wisdom" (Ps. 90:12 NKJV).

Our view of time is bound by the cultural context we find ourselves in and is dictated by what that culture values. As an American living in Mexico, I will never forget the first party my family was invited to. It was for a quinceañera, and we were told it would start at 3:00 p.m. We made the typical American rush to have the kids ready to go, budgeting the time to drive over long, dirt roads to arrive a little earlier than the 3:00 start time. When we arrived, we were met by the family who had clearly not even begun getting ready for the event. It was then that we learned that start time meant it was time to start getting ready, and the actual party wouldn't begin for another couple of hours. While we arrived "on time," others were just getting in the shower and preparing for the event. As for when the event would end, we were given just a shrug and a "we'll see." This culture was clearly operating under a different understanding of time than we were. If this is true cross-culturally, it stands to reason that time in God's courts also moves differently than in our home. When you compound that with a cultural norm of instant everything, it can be very frustrating when things don't seem to be moving at the pace we want.

There are seasons in our lives when we learn something new about God or ourselves and are given opportunities to practice

---

90. See Ps. 90:12.

it right away. Praise God when we can clearly see the cause and effect. Yet there are other seasons that require detoxing from an adrenaline rush in order to slow our hearts and minds. These seasons do not typically offer the effect directly from the cause but invite us to evaluate both. God desires to lead us into deeper places of our soul that require healing, which is always a slow, still work that happens over time. Instead of overlaying our time frame for when we would like this work to begin and end, we submit ourselves to the long, arduous process that doesn't offer any easy fixes or answers. We can be sure that when these are being withheld from us, God is going to begin a great new work in us. What is required is simply a willingness to develop patience, practice grace for ourselves and others, and pray for recognition of the presence of God.

2. A Season of Listening

"In the multitude of words sin is not lacking, but he who restrains his lips *is* wise" (Prov. 10:19 NKJV). What strikes me about that familiar proverb is how true it is across the board. For someone who uses his words for a living, I bristle at it, thinking of the multitude of words my job requires in teaching, writing, counseling, and coaching. In the last few years, I have experienced an overhaul of what I understand my job as a pastor to be in light of this. Instead of being the Bible answer man with golden-tongued wisdom pouring from my lips, I find myself listening a lot more. Instead of being the CEO of a religious organization, I have been tasked with paying attention to where Jesus is, what He might be saying, and how He may be leading me and those around me. That gives me pause, and instead of rushing in to boldly proclaim "thus saith the Lord," I just want to become a little more still and quiet first.

Truly listening to others leads to asking a lot of questions rather than giving answers, which often leads to deeper work under the surface that I may have been unaware of. Active waiting for God not only requires time but involves a lot of listening. Perhaps the most difficult part of this stage is discerning what voices we are listening to. When we begin to desire to become better listeners, we first pay attention to the number of voices clambering for our attention. As Henri Nouwen said, "Our inner life is like a banana tree filled with monkeys jumping up and down. It is not easy to sit and trust that in solitude God will speak to us."[91] At any given time, when I decide to quiet my heart and mind before the Lord, I become aware of all the voices in my life telling me what to do, how to do it, how wrong I am, how great I am, what a fool I am for trying to attempt some new work, and how I am failing my wife, my children, and my friends. I have voices from old seminary professors clucking their disapproval for seeking such a mystical communion with God instead of simply reading His Word. I have voices from my family of origin telling me who I need to be, yet other voices from an earlier version of myself are telling me to relax. On top of that, I have deceptive voices from the enemy of my soul telling me it's too late, all is lost, I'm worthless, and my sin is too great for God to forgive.

Quieting ourselves is much harder in practice than it is in theory.

So we begin by heeding St. Paul's advice to "take every thought captive to obey Christ" (2 Cor. 10:5). We test these voices against what we know to be the will of God and dismiss those clearly not leading to power, love, and a sound mind.[92] We lean into John

---

91. Henri J. M. Nouwen, *A Spirituality of Living* (Nashville, TN: Upper Room, 2012), 3.
92. See 2 Tim. 1:7.

10, knowing that the Good Shepherd knows us and we will listen to His voice. The self-authenticating voice of Jesus resonates so deeply in the hearts of those who have been sealed by His Spirit that we know what sounds like our Savior's voice, bringing peace and rest even in the midst of the struggle. Any voice that leads me to deepen my trust in Jesus and deepen my desire for Jesus alone is a voice worth listening to.

Gem Fadling from Unhurried Living has developed a helpful tool to help us place our bodies in a physical state of listening as we align our hearts with a posture of listening. We first find a quiet place for ourselves and then practice breathing deeply, paying attention to inhaling grace and exhaling thankfulness. We practice an inner stillness that waits on our Father to be near us. Fadling then uses the acronym BREATHE. You may want to give it a trial run as you're reading this. Slow down for a moment, and work your way through this acronym.

Be: Be present exactly where you are, not somewhere else, not sometime else. Be here now.

Relax: Relax your shoulders, your eyes, your mind, your body. Pay attention to any hesitancy to do so.

Encounter: Encounter God, remembering that you are not alone. God is not somewhere else; He is with you right here and right now.

Attend: Attend to your emotions. Are you anxious? Are you joyful? Are you sad? Do you feel rushed? Frustrated? Excited? God is with you as you feel this.

Thank: Thank God for being with you. Thank Him for this moment of rest. Thank God for reminding you to pause. Thank Him for whatever you're feeling. It is His way of getting your attention.

Help: Ask God for help. Did a need surface? How about an unwelcome emotion? Ask God for help, for you are not alone. Trust God to care for you.

Engage: Engage your life with more peace, with a lighter heart. Reenter a relationship with a little more perspective. Engage from a place of grace.[93]

Don't you already feel a little more relaxed? Is your mind a little clearer? Is your heart a little more hopeful? That is what the presence of God does, and listening is how we place ourselves under the shelter of His wings.

3. A Season of Reflection

Active waiting requires both time and a posture of listening, two elements that form the nutrients from which healthy things can grow. Reflection is how we cultivate that soil, knowing what to prune, dig up, or help grow. This is a more difficult part since it requires a brutal honesty with yourself and a gospel big enough to offer hope in the darkest places of your heart. Socrates is said to have uttered, "The unexamined life is not worth living."[94] More poetically, the musical artist Sleeping at Last sings, "We'll build new traditions in place of the old / 'Cause life without revision will silence our souls."[95]

Reflection is how we examine various facets of our life—where we've been, who we are, who we would like to be, and how we get

93. Gem Fadling, "Podcast 19: BREATHE – A 6 Minute Retreat," September 25, 2017, in *Unhurried Living*, podcast, 6:53, https://www.unhurriedliving.com/blog/podcast19. The acronym is taken from Fadling; the explanations are my paraphrases.

94. "The Unexamined Life Is Not Worth Living," School Work Helper, accessed July 9, 2021, https://schoolworkhelper.net/quote-analysis-the-unexamined-life-is-not-worth-living/.

95. "Snow," Written by Ryan O'Neal. ©2011 Wine and Song Music (BMI) on behalf of itself & Asteroid B-612. International Copyright Secured All Rights Reserved. Used By Permission.

there. We can begin by reflecting on our actions and then let those actions lead us downward into our hearts. This is not unlike the Daily Examen developed by St. Ignatius where we pay attention to consolations (where God came to us that day) and desolations (things that drew us away from God that day). For example, as I was reflecting on my day some time ago, I remembered a meeting I had with a staff member that caused me to become frustrated. She was asking me questions I didn't have the answers to, and I felt frustrated with myself for not being able to answer reasonable questions.

Recognizing those feelings is awareness, but even deeper under that frustration is a big lie that forms so much of what I think or feel. I believed that if I did not have the answers to everyone's questions or could not fix every situation, I was a worthless human being. Even deeper than that lie is an abiding sense of insecurity that leads me to overidentify with my gifts to alleviate my own perceived deficiency. What led me away from God was my own script that if I could not provide excellent services for another at all times, I had no value. Even saying that out loud in the presence of God sounds like a lie, and I can now go to Scripture to tell me who I am in Him at all times—both when I am performing well and when I am not. I am a cherished son, beloved of the Father who desires me to rest in the perfection of Jesus, given to me at great cost to Him. There is nothing I can do to make Him love me more, and there is nothing I can do to make Him love me less. Armed with that knowledge in my soul, my response to my employee could have been humbler and gracious. Since I could not go back in time to change my actions, what was left was to apologize, acknowledge why I responded the way I did, and learn from that the next time.

If that example and train of thought sound overwhelming to you, let me suggest starting small. I was in my late 30s before I could confidently state how I felt about anything. I was working with a fourth-grade vocabulary to describe my emotions—sad, mad, bad, glad. I simply did not have access to a breadth of descriptive language to express myself. When it came to talking about what I thought, I excelled and thus naturally assumed that when I was asked how I felt about something, it was synonymous with what I thought about it. A pastor friend of mine sent me a chart called "the emotion wheel," which is exactly what it sounds like. Beginning with the six to eight primary emotions (depending on what chart you look at), it extrapolates subsections of emotions underneath each one. For example, under "Fearful" is a second level of clarifying emotions—scared, anxious, insecure, weak, rejected, threatened. Under each of those words is a third level of clarifying emotions. Instead of scared, are we feeling helpless or frightened? With no right answer, we are free to become curious about ourselves, our feelings, and the causes for them. I would quiet myself every morning, afternoon, and evening, pull out my printed copy of the wheel, and begin to make check marks next to the emotion that described how I felt. After doing that for some time, I could visually see what areas of the wheel I tended to identify with more than others. After several months of this practice, I began to integrate a fuller emotional language into my mental framework and life. You can check out the chart on the next page and begin practicing it.

This and other practices like it are how we take inventory of our souls. Self-reflection helps us see what things are at play under the surface in our lives that lead us to think, speak, and act the way we do. Even this is a great grace to our humanity, lifting us up to the heavenlies where every spiritual blessing is already ours.[96]

---

96. See Eph. 1:3.

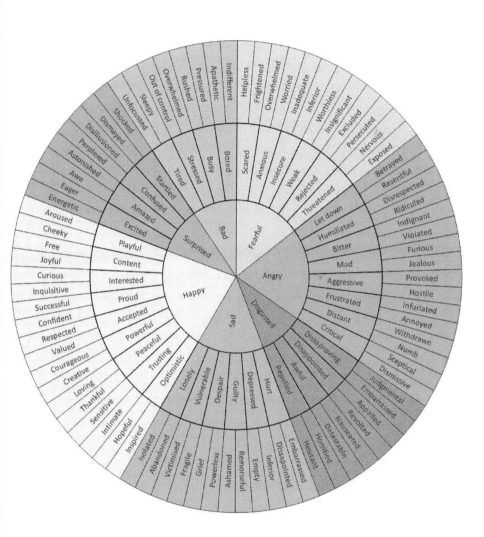

I have an all-or-nothing personality, which at its best leads me to take risks with great faith. At its worst, it prevents me from acknowledging my faults. If I am wrong in something, I must be wrong in everything. That lie is too much for my soul to bear. So I spin the truth and turn a negative into a positive to believe the lie that I never make mistakes, or at least mistakes that aren't as bad as other people's. One of the greatest consolations that has come from extended seasons of waiting for the Lord is the affirmation that only Jesus is perfect, and my humanity requires an acknowledgment that I am dust, a frail, faulty human being full of incredible selfishness and sin as well as incredible faith, trust, and love. That is what it means to be human.

You can begin practicing this self-reflection by asking some of the above questions in the BREATHE exercise. What are you anxious about in your life? Why are you anxious? What are you afraid will happen? Then start to dig a little deeper in silence before the Lord, asking Him for wisdom to uncover why you feel that way. Where does it come from? Is it a habitual thought or reflexive action for you? Does it come from your family of origin? Does it come from a previous failure you haven't come to terms with? Let Jesus lead your time, speaking healing into these areas.

4. A Season of Observation

Instead of looking only inward, doing the long work of self-reflection, we can also pay attention to external observations about our lives. Planned liminality means taking an active role in waiting for God as we come to terms with reality—the life we have been given to live. For most of us, there is or will be a period in life when the sum of all we have done and lived comes back to us. Robert Southey once said that chickens "always come home to roost."[97] We are faced with deep regrets over dreams that will never come to pass, missed opportunities, and a growing list of losses, sorrows, and limits. Not one of us has ever been able to craft the life for ourselves we thought we wanted. Instead, we are left with wins and losses, good times and bad times, sadness and joys all mixed together. Wisdom leads us to an honest evaluation of our part in this, as well as the circumstances God has allowed to shape us into the people we are today. I have a handwritten note on my desk of a quote from one of my spiritual directors that I look at every day. It says, "The ideal situation in which to grow spiritually is your life right now, exactly as you find it."[98] This helps center my external observation away from despair and regret into a more hopeful place of entering my actual life as the environment God wants to use to make me more like Jesus. The more I steep myself in the reality of Philippians 3, the more I, too, count everything as loss for the sake of knowing Christ and being found in Him, both in His resurrection power and in the fellowship of His sufferings.[99] What is true of my life today—the good, the bad, and the ugly—can serve in knowing the work and person of Jesus, which is a greater joy than all else.

Another meaningful observation to make is noting areas of great good and blessing in our lives that we did nothing to earn.

---

97. "The Chickens Come Home to Roost," Well-Known Expressions, BookBrowse, accessed June 22, 2021, https://www.bookbrowse.com/expressions/detail/index.cfm/expression_number/183/the-chickens-come-home-to-roost.

98. From a conversation with Alan Fadling of Unhurried Living. See Gem Fadling and Alan Fadling, *What Does Your Soul Love?: Eight Questions That Reveal God's Work in You* (Downers Grove, IL: InterVarsity Press, 2019), 138.

99. See Phil. 3:10.

That may be the unconditional love of a wife you do not deserve or a dream job that landed in your lap without even looking for it. It may be some natural ability or spiritual gift that allows you to create something beautiful in the world. From having enough food to eat, to good health that allows us to enjoy mobility, to the simple joys of a warm summer evening with friends, there are always blessings waiting for you to count. Sometimes they are ever before us as a muse for our worship, and other times we may have to look harder for the light through the trees, but evidence of God's grace is *always* around us.

On a somewhat darker note, we also observe areas of our life where things are not what we hoped they would be. Maybe we have a strained relationship with someone close to us or a lack of joy in our work. Without initially making value judgments, we simply observe different aspects where we may be unhappy with our lives. We may have bad habits that have crept in over the years, poor rhythms of overwork and inability to rest, or unhealthy addictions we use to numb our pain. By God's grace, we can offer these to God and ask Him for help to understand when they began and why. We then seek God's help to overcome them by building healthier patterns in our lives.

At other times, God is bringing us into an experience of desolation in order to renew our sense of need for Him and bring us back to Himself as the source of all life. There is biblical precedent for this in the book of Amos. In chapter 4, God says He was responsible for a famine, but His people did not return to Him. Then He sent them a drought, but they did not return to Him. He sent a blight on their crops, but they did not return to Him. Then he sent sickness and finally war, but still they did not return to Him. God was responsible for bringing these hardships on His people for a purpose—that they would turn from their sin, seek God, and live.[100] The prophet Isaiah explicitly tells Israel to wait on the Lord in the path of His judgments. "For when your judgments are in the earth, the inhabitants of the world learn righteousness" (Isa. 26:9). Finally, it is worth quoting Lamentations since it mirrors many of our personal experiences during times of desolation. While we may not have experienced the actual physical destruction of our cities, homes, and families in the way the Israelites did when Jerusalem fell to the Babylonian army, we have all experienced similar feelings during difficult times.

> *I am the man who has seen affliction under the rod of his wrath; he has driven and brought me into darkness without any light; surely against me he turns his hand again and again the whole day long. . . . He has walled me about so that I cannot escape; he has made my chains heavy; though I call and cry for help, he shuts out my prayer; he has blocked my ways with blocks of stones; he has made my paths crooked. . . . He has filled me with bitterness. . . . My soul is bereft of peace; I have forgotten what happiness is; so I say, "My endurance has perished; so has my hope from the LORD."*
>
> —Lam. 3:1–3, 7–9, 15, 17–18

Heavy stuff, that. If Jeremiah was indeed the author of the book, he was a man of sorrows during his entire ministry to the kingdom that was in decline. In this passage, he is finally sitting in the ashes of Jerusalem watching God do what He promised to do if they would not repent and return. So much of his language is familiar to those who have waited for the Lord during hard times. Whether due to our own sin, circumstances beyond our control, or walking

---

100. See Amos 4:6–11.

with those we love during their periods of crisis and turmoil, Jeremiah's feelings of bitterness, aimlessness, and anger at God ring true. When we are being forced to wait, it can feel as if God were blocking our path, shutting out our prayers, and ignoring our pain.

Incredibly, Jeremiah's lament does not end there. He was a man who knew that God can be known through suffering as well as resurrection, so he continues:

> But this I call to mind, and therefore I have hope: The steadfast love of the LORD never ceases; his mercies never come to an end; they are new every morning; great is your faithfulness. "The LORD is my portion," says my soul, "therefore I will hope in him." The LORD is good to those who wait for him, to the soul who seeks him. It is good that one should wait quietly for the salvation of the LORD. . . . For the Lord will not cast off forever, but, though he cause grief, he will have compassion according to the abundance of his steadfast love; for he does not afflict from his heart or grieve the children of men. . . . Let us test and examine our ways, and return to the LORD!
>
> —Lam. 3:21–26, 31–33, 40

I don't know if it is more comforting to have shared Jeremiah's feeling of abandonment during seasons of desolation or more convicting that I did not share his sense of God's goodness until much, much later. Jeremiah is living in the midst of the tension between desolation and consolation in a way I long for. This lengthy passage from Lamentations reinforces the prophet's insistence that at times God does use hardship to bring us back to Him. When we are experiencing His judgments, we learn righteousness. We have been talking about externally observing our lives during seasons of waiting. It is not only possible but probable that God might be using this period to refine us by reminding us of our need for Him. Even the Ephesian church, praised in the book of Revelation for their good works, had to be reminded that they had abandoned the love they had for Jesus at first. John's counsel to them was to "remember therefore from where you have fallen; repent, and do the works you did at first" (Rev. 2:5).

Seasons of intense pain, loss, and suffering are the most fertile times for us to encounter the God who saves. Being able to do nothing but wait reminds us of our humanity and teaches us to lift up our eyes and see where our help comes from, even if we are unable to see how to do that just yet. The caveat here, and this is a big one, is that until we truly and thoroughly value knowing Jesus above all, through whatever means possible, it is likely we will not have the strength to endure the pain that brings us to Him. We will focus only on the suffering, the difficulty, the first half of Jeremiah's lament, without ever allowing it to cause us to return to the Lord and renew our affection and desire for Him. C. S. Lewis was right when he wrote, "Pain insists upon being attended to. God whispers to us in our pleasures, speaks in our conscience, but shouts in our pain. It is His megaphone to rouse a deaf world."[101]

Remember that it is pure grace to have the ability to meditate on our ways. Waiting for God is the way we pay attention to the deep things of our hearts and souls. Pursuing this level of inner work will pay dividends we would not believe if we let patience have its perfect work so we "may be perfect and complete, lacking in nothing" (James 1:4).

---

101. C. S. Lewis, *The Problem of Pain* (New York: HarperCollins Publishers, 1940), 91.

Φ

CHAPTER EIGHT: SELF-EXAMINATION

You were more inward to me than my most inward part and higher than my highest.

—Augustine

For you formed my inward parts; you knitted me together in my mother's womb . . . My frame was not hidden from you, when I was being made in secret, intricately woven in the depths of the earth. Your eyes saw my unformed substance.

—Ps. 139:13–16

You have traveled too fast over false ground;
Now your soul has come to take you back.

Take refuge in your senses, open up
To all the small miracles you rushed through.

Become inclined to watch the way of rain
When it falls slow and free. . . .

Be excessively gentle with yourself.

—John O'Donohue

Like all times of experiential learning, the forced discipline of waiting helps synchronize what is happening in our bodies with what is happening in our minds as we try to make some kind of emotional sense of where we are and what we are feeling. When we slow down and allow the weight of liminality to wash over us, it is not uncommon for less desirable feelings and emotions to rise to the surface. Many times, they come to us in the form of shame. As we learn to enjoy more time of silence and solitude, we meet Jesus in the hidden places of our lives. He graciously brings to the surface things that our incessant busyness was hiding from us and allows us the time to feel the attending emotions. Rather than being able to move on to the next activity, project, or chore, we can choose to stay with the uncomfortable thoughts and emotions. As we sit with our less desirable emotions, Jesus speaks to us, inviting us to bring that shame and guilt to Him. Psychologists and authors Alison Cook and Kimberly Miller remind us that "burdens of shame do not define you. Whereas these lies say you are unimportant, God says you are decidedly well-known and deeply loved. And you can be real because you are his. You are the light of the world—and shame has no place in the light."[102]

Listening to Jesus speak truth over us can be the greatest gift of God during periods of waiting if we develop ears to hear it. Our lives are constantly numbed by the amount of activities, words, noise, and responsibilities that land at our doorstep in a single day. By rushing from one thing to the next, we anesthetize our souls to the presence of Jesus, the one thing that is necessary. It doesn't just happen with the mindless busyness that comes with having school-aged children where every night of the week is

---

102. Alison Cook, PhD and Kimberly Miller, MTh, LMFT, *Boundaries for Your Soul: How to Turn Your Overwhelming Thoughts and Feelings into Your Greatest Allies* (New York: HarperCollins, 2018), 193.

spent driving all over town to recitals, practices, banquets, sports games, and the like. It can also happen through an incessant amount of self-imposed religious noise and teaching.

I recently became aware of a bad habit I have. When I'm listening to a really good podcast, I keep playing the next, then the next, then the next until all the silent spaces of the day have been eaten away by more teaching, instruction, information, and trivia. Instead of stopping to digest what I just heard, leaving room to savor and enjoy it, I fill the empty space with more noise. Thus, all the natural pauses in my day—driving in the car, walking to a meeting, cooking a meal, or doing the dishes— all become means of avoidance. Instead, they should be times of reflection about where my body and soul are, inviting Jesus into that and becoming content with the silence from which the voice of God can speak. I limit the voice of God to what I hear from a podcast, a sermon, a book, or a family member, but I don't give Him much of a chance to speak to me directly. How vain are the things we spend our life to save!

The act of choosing to pause, reflect, and pay attention to ourselves and Jesus is the way we examine ourselves. Through it, we pay attention to things our bodies and souls have been trying to tell us, sometimes through sickness, chronic fatigue, or headaches. At other times, this invitation comes through an unmet longing in our hearts for more or a dark night of depression that clouds our judgment and thought life, casting a shadow over things that should bring joy. As we pay attention to body and soul, we move toward God, inviting the presence of the Holy Spirit to illuminate what is going on under the surface of our lives. We invite Jesus to show us where He has been walking with us throughout the day or week. Then we meditate on what God might be trying to tell us through it all. These three movements—pausing, paying attention to ourselves, and paying attention to God—are the hard work of self-examination. Let's take a look at how to establish these movements as a regular practice.

First Movement: Pausing

At times, the gift of waiting on God comes through the complete inability to do anything but wait. Try as we may, there seems to be no forward movement, no opportunities for action, and we can do nothing but wait. At first we may rage at the circumstances that caused a season of waiting, but eventually we are left shadow boxing ourselves with no resolution to the fight. Once our arms are tired from punching those we blame, our minds are tired from trying to figure out how we got into this mess, and our hearts are tired of feeling so helpless and useless, then we can begin the work of pausing.

Before we pause to reflect, pray, read, or think, we must simply stop whatever we're doing. We intentionally allow our body posture to reflect the lack of activity in every other area of our lives. Ironically, for a faith tradition that worships a God who literally took on flesh (*incaros*) and lived in a human body, we are unaccustomed to paying much attention to our own. Incorporating our physical bodies with our spiritual growth seems strange and at odds with each other, so we neglect the gift of our bodies. This has been called "mindfulness," as good a word as any to describe our awareness of the present moment as an embodied soul, allowing ourselves to pay attention to our physical location (sounds, smells, and sights) as well as our emotional and mental state (feelings, emotions, and thoughts).

A surprising entrance into pausing is through play. Play serves most often as a catalyst, forcing us to take stock of why we don't do it more. The mental, physical, and emotional benefits of play are well-documented. In his excellent book *Play*, Stuart Brown defines play as any kind of purposeless, all-consuming, restorative activity and claims that it is the single most significant factor in determining our success and happiness.[103] Play serves as a catalyst for pausing because it requires us to shift our mental energies from productivity and efficiency to seemingly non-essential behaviors. Playing forces us to press pause on our busy lives to indulge in something life-giving. It looks different for each of us, but we know an activity is a gateway to pausing and resting when it truly is something all-consuming for us. Whether it is music, gardening, woodworking, or reading a good novel, it rejuvenates us. Perhaps most importantly, play requires neither skill nor ability, and we all come as amateurs, not professionals.

I'm an active person with a lot of energy to burn off when I'm healthy, so a lot of my play is very physical. I'm ashamed to say that when I was first asked years ago what I liked to do for fun, I had no answer. Think about that for a moment. I was so unhealthy that not only did I have no hobbies but I could not identify a single life-giving activity I could pursue. Maybe that's you right now. If so, the very idea of pausing is likely threatening, much less having a plan to practice it. I still have my first list I ever tried to make of things I enjoyed. It consisted of naps and beer. But I made a point to pay attention and keep my eyes open. Later that year, I took my first sabbatical in 16 years of full-time ministry. My family left Los Angeles for an epic road trip and traveled across the country to visit friends, national parks, and places we'd never been. During one of our stops in Austin, Texas, some friends took us to the river for the afternoon. After eating lunch at Franklin Barbecue (if you're ever in Austin, go

---

103. Stuart Brown, M.D., *Play* (New York: The Penguin Group, 2009), 6.

there), we brought some snacks, a kayak, and swim trunks to play in the river for the day. At some point on this warm summer day, it started to rain—pouring rain in a way we're not used to in Los Angeles. Most of my family left to go back to the place we were staying with a friend, but one of my sons, our friend, and I decided to stay. At some point, I recall being in the kayak, on the water, in the rain, and feeling more *alive* than I had felt in a long time. I was feeling the water on my skin, listening to the water hit more water, and tasting the water in my mouth. It took copious amounts of water in all directions for me to realize I loved being on the water, in the water, around the water. Rivers, lakes, the ocean, even little creeks that only have water when it rains by us—it doesn't matter. What's more, I realized my soul had always known this; I had just not stopped long enough to pay attention.

I started thinking back on some of the most joyful trips I had taken, and there was always some element of water or water sports. I thought back to a whitewater rafting trip when I was a teenager. I remembered beach days in the summer when I spent hours in the ocean, not on the beach. I recalled my childhood and how excited I was when we moved to California and could actually have a pool in our backyard. All this came from stopping long enough to play and think. When we got back home from that trip, I bought a paddleboard and began spending as much time as I could in the ocean. Water isn't just my happy place where I feel the most alive; it's also a place where once I'm past the break, there's nothing to do but paddle, think, and enjoy the view. It's a life-giving activity that also has a built-in pause to it. Why don't you try some playful activity yourself and see if it leads to more time to pause? You'd be amazed how much awareness can come from simply pausing your doing in order to focus on your being.

Second Movement: Paying Attention to Ourselves

In AD 500, Augustine wrote in his *Confessions*, "How can you draw close to God when you are so far from yourself?" More than 1,000 years later, theologian John Calvin agreed. "Our wisdom consists almost entirely of two parts: the knowledge of God and of ourselves. But as these are connected together by many ties, it is not easy to determine which of the two precedes and gives birth to the other."[104]

If we are not accustomed to paying attention to the inner world of our soul, we run the risk of never living the life Jesus gave us to live and instead chase after something we were told we should value (the American dream) or live for someone else's expectations of us. How, indeed, do we expect to know God with any depth or reality if we are unaware of the self He fashioned for us to be able to perceive Him with? I am only able to experience a relationship with God in Christ through His Spirit that indwells the physical body He has given me. This body is the only way I have walked through life, first as a child, then as an adolescent, and now as a man. With my own set of strengths and weaknesses, limitations, and gifts, I have learned how to perceive the world around me. I have also lived most of my life aware of these unique attributes only tangentially as I discovered I was unable to do something athletic or excel at some intellectual pursuit. Not being in touch with who and whose we are leaves us living someone else's life.

Paying attention to ourselves is actually more an exercise in paying attention to our *selves*. Family therapist Dr. Richard Schwartz developed Internal Family Systems in response to his clients' descriptions of experiencing various parts within themselves, forming an internal family within an individual. Over

---

104. John Calvin, *The Institutes of the Christian Religion*, Translated by Henry Beveridge (Peabody, MA: Hendrickson Publishers, 2008), 4.

time, he identified at least three consistent and common "selves" that existed within each person—the Manager, the Firefighter, and the Exile. All these parts are good, needed, and helpful when we're functioning properly. If we're living improperly, one of these aspects can be given disproportionate attention, use unhealthy means of accomplishing goals, or be repressed, ignored, and left to fester. The Exile is that part of our selves that is vulnerable, often carries wounds and past traumas, and isolates from the rest of the family to protect us from feeling pain, terror, fear, and more. The Manager is that part of our selves that runs our day-to-day lives and attempts to keep us in control and protect the other parts from hurt or rejection. The Firefighter is that part of our selves that re-acts when we are feeling the shame and hurt of the Exile by numb-ing and avoiding. It is responsible for our coping mechanisms and strategies. Paying attention to our selves means being aware of and listening to all the different parts of our selves. We pay attention to each of these parts since they are equally true and can be equally helpful when our True Self brings them into submission.

Once we identify that each of these parts are in play, we can become curious about them, asking questions of them, acknowledging our feelings about them, and ultimately showing grace to each aspect of our selves to find more positive ways to be in the world. This is a helpful way to begin the practice of paying attention to our selves by knowing the feelings, thoughts and sensations that drive us. Think about all the energy we spend feeling shame and berating ourselves for being sexually abused as a child (Exile). Think of the attention we give to the sensation of needing release, the danger of numbing ourselves in order to get what our souls need (Firefighter). And think of the amount of time we spend creating mental maps and strategies to be successful in our lives (Manager). By getting to know each version of our self, we can make those selves allies and advisors, bringing integrity, internal stability, and peace to our lives.

This type of inner work is how we build on our structured pauses and incorporate curiosity. Part of the reason we typically keep ourselves busy, running at an unsustainable pace, is that we are afraid (and unaware of our fear) of what would rise to the surface if we let it. But instead of allowing our inner critic or unhealthy Firefighter to have the final word over our emotions, we can become curious, holding those emotions at a distance to examine them. Rather than detachment, let yourself feel what you feel, but get curious about why you are feeling it. If everything is going well, why are you feeling anxious? Without passing judgment, hitting your feelings with a Bible verse, or pretending they're not real, just ask better questions. Because you are feeling something doesn't make it true, but it does mean God might be trying to get your attention through those feelings. Without trying too hard to figure out the mysteries of the universe or your soul, just sit with all these emotions. They don't have the final word over what is true about you, but it's easy to listen to them nonetheless.

During a recent season of practicing these concepts, I became aware that shame was the loudest emotion in my life. As I went through my day, I started to make a list of all the times I felt shame. When I saw that a peer was invited to teach at a conference instead of me, I believed it was clearly because I didn't have what it takes. Or the time I texted another pastor to get to know him better, only to be met with silence. It was obvious that it was because I was uninteresting and unimportant. As I thought about the different events in my day, I gradually became aware of how steeped my soul was in berating myself, believing the worst about myself, and living as if everyone else were doing the same. As I spent a little more time on this, I peeled another layer off that emotion and linked it to my familiar defensiveness when approached about a wrongdoing, a mistake, or outright hurting someone else. I felt so guilty and ashamed most of the time that my soul couldn't handle hearing another bad thing about myself, and thus I became defensive. That was a big realization that came from simply stopping long enough to pay attention to what was going on inside of me.

Another time, my wife asked me a clarifying question about a speaking engagement, and I snapped at her. I then spent the next hour or two being frustrated and angry, wallowing in my bad attitude. Then I started asking questions. Why was I so quick with my wife? I had been having a good morning, but a string of reasonable questions from her set me off. What about the speaking engagement was I frustrated about? By paying attention, I remembered a previous email. I had been asked to lead a specific portion of a retreat and then given a list of ideas, videos, worksheets, and sermon notes that I thought I needed to incorporate. I was feeling like there were expectations that weren't clarified, and the person in charge would rather have done it themselves in order to do it just right. I often respond negatively to the feeling of being controlled. I am fine giving over leadership roles and positions, but I hate the thought of being controlled by someone else. There's a host of reasons for this—a detached attachment pattern, having more trust in myself than someone else, and the way I equate independence with freedom. None of these strategies serve me particularly well any longer, and by getting curious and asking questions, I was better able to mitigate their control of me. Either we take ownership and responsibility for our own story, or the pain that comes from it will own us, often without even being aware of it. The truth will set us free, indeed.

There is another piece, a danger, really, of paying attention to our selves. Unless we have come to value and practice self-compassion, the voice of our inner critic is likely stronger than any other. We are never as gentle with our weaknesses as Jesus is with them. Do you know what your inner critic sounds like? Is it the distant father telling you you're never enough? Maybe it's the voices of the popular girls in high school who assure you that you did not wear enough makeup to be pretty, you were too curvy or not curvy enough, or any number of insecurities. For some of us, the inner critic sounds like the coach who can't accept defeat and tells us "you got this" even when it's clearly time to throw in the towel. Whatever the tone or content of your critic, that voice typically does not speak truth, or if it does, it certainly doesn't speak it in love. The voice of our inner critic plays off our latent anxieties and amplifies what is already under the surface. Just know that when the Spirit of God desires to convict, He always does it with tenderness and gentleness. When God moves toward us in our shame, he is warm and inquisitive, often asking questions rather than making pronouncements. Jesus asked us to come to Him and learn from Him because He is gentle and humble in heart.[105] The ability to cut through the judgment of the wrong voices and focus on the right one leads us to the third movement.

Third Movement: Paying Attention to God

As we become more aware, paying attention to our inner dialogue must move us outward to hear the voice of Jesus that speaks a better word over us.[106] Therapist and author K. J. Ramsey says this:

> *Learning to inhabit our new selves—the life "hidden with Christ in God"—will take time, will feel like*

---

105. See Matt. 11:29.
106. See Heb. 12:24.

losing control, and will require our attention. Though our old self has been crucified with Christ, it will take time for our old brain to die. The silent narrator of shame will keep whispering that safety is in the shadows, but in Christ we can listen to and respond to the voice of God's love calling us to light.[107]

Paying attention to God means bravely practicing what He has already told us is true in His Word, not what we feel is true in any given moment. This is actually what it looks like to walk by faith, not by sight, and it is not simply reading, knowing, and memorizing the Word of God, although that is part of it. It is ingesting it into the deepest parts of our lives until God shapes us from the inside out. When God called the prophet Ezekiel, He told him He had hard words for the nation of Israel that they would not receive. He then gave the prophet a scroll with His words on it to eat. Ezekiel tells us that there were written words of lamentation, mourning, and woe on the scroll. He was to feed his stomach and the deepest parts with this scroll. When he ate the scroll, it was as sweet as honey in his mouth.[108] The Apostle John had a similar experience eating a scroll in the book of Revelation, using similar imagery. He was told it would be sweet as honey in his mouth but bitter in his stomach. He ate it, or literally devoured it, which meant he received it into himself.[109]

Paying attention to God in our waiting requires more than reading a book or listening to a podcast. It means actually spending time with the Father in the presence of the Spirit,

107. K. J. Ramsey, *This Too Shall Last: Finding Grace When Suffering Lingers* (Grand Rapids, MI: Zondervan, 2020), 168.
108. See Ezek. 2:8–3:11.
109. See Rev. 10:1–11.

empowered by the freedom of the gospel the Son brings. We no longer need to hide from anything since the gospel is a daily reminder that Christ already died for the worst parts of ourselves to be redeemed. We then choose to live and walk in the light, naked and unashamed. As Frederick Buechner said, "The hardest thing about really seeing and really hearing is that then we really have to do something about what we have seen and heard."[110] What has God been trying to bring to your attention? It bears repeating that when God brings hard things to our attention, He does so gently with a tenderness we so rarely know how to give to ourselves. This tenderness distinguishes His voice from imposters who want to steal, condemn, and destroy. Walking in newness of life always requires doing hard things and establishing different patterns of relating to God, ourselves, and others.

This requires the Word of God, not as a plumb line of morality but as the means to know the heart of God. This way of reading Scripture sometimes means rethinking how we have heard and ingested the Word of God in the past. For instance, when you hear the phrase "gifts of God," what do you initially think of? Is it the spiritual gifts Paul speaks of or the good gifts of God that Jesus spoke of? The spiritual gifts are those imparted to us on behalf of others. The good gifts of the Father are meant for us as recipients to enjoy. One is for the furtherance of the Kingdom of God; the other is for our own nourishment.[111] Paying attention to God first means paying attention to our relationship with Him, not our work for Him.

---

110. Frederick Buechner, What's My Quote?, accessed June 22, 2021, https://whatsmyquote.com/quote/the-trouble-with-really-seeing-and-really-hearing-is-that-then-we-really-have-to-do-something-about-what-we/page/4.

111. I'm indebted to Pastor Steve Cuss from Capable Life for this question. Steve Cuss, *Managing Leadership Anxiety: Yours and Theirs* (Nashville, TN: Thomas Nelson, 2019), 129.

The Word of God often contradicts the inner critic and leads us to become "excessively gentle with ourselves," to borrow O'Donohue's phrase. The gentler we learn to become with our humanity, the more room we make for God's divinity to invade our humanity. We become deeply aware that we need a divine word to guide our steps. We feel our brokenness deeply and our need for divine strength to lift up our feeble bodies. Our thinking, which we like to feel was untouched by the fall, allowing us to competently survey our landscape, becomes faulty and unreliable, making room for divine wisdom to help us walk by faith. In short, we repent of our desire for reasonableness, control, and governance of our own lives and look to the One humbly born as a child with the government on His mighty shoulders.

Here is the trap. Good, sound doctrine is meant to lead us to a *real* encounter with the living God, not a *right* one. The more we cling to doctrine to make us right, satisfy our desire for control, and trick ourselves into believing we are, in fact, masters of divinity, the more likely it will be that we won't have a real encounter. For some of us, sound doctrine is not the means to the end; it is the box we must stay inside of in order to be safe. Exercising a good desire to rightly handle the word of truth[112] and not be led astray by every wind of false doctrine,[113] we can be tempted to trade the love of Jesus for His cold approval of how well we understand facts about Him.

Let me illustrate these ideas. When I first came to Jesus, I believed reincarnation was a biblical doctrine. After all, having been steeped in worldly wisdom for more than 20 years, I found it a hard concept to escape. During my first six months as a

---

112. See 2 Tim. 2:15.
113. See Eph. 4:14.

follower of Jesus, I naturally fit reincarnation into everything I was learning about God. I was perfectly loved by Jesus in that moment. I meant that. God does not love or approve of me more now when I have superior knowledge of Him than when I was my 24-year-old self. Even my wrong but pure belief about something that was the antithesis of the cross did not make Jesus cringe. He still fiercely loved me in the same way a parent fiercely loves a child who has an irrational fear of the dark or believes in an imaginary friend. Time and maturity will displace such fantasies as they did many of my false beliefs. I became convinced of the contradiction by reading the Bible,[114] cross-referencing passages that spoke of judgment, and using the brand-new framework of a Christian worldview to help me make sense of the world around me and the life to come. Understanding the nuanced interplay of judgment and grace, wrath and love, faith and works did not make me more loved, desired, or smarter than my friends. It simply helped me rest even more deeply in the unbelievable love and goodness of God. The doctrine led to an encounter with God.

As a pastor, I have a front-row seat to watch religious people grasp the gospel for the very first time. It displaces their logical legalism, their cold religious devotion for the story of God traveling across time and space and heaven and hell to rescue His beloved. It is like watching the scales fall from someone's eyes as they see familiar shapes and outlines clearly for the first time. It never gets old. It frees them from trying to impress God to simply resting in His presence, wanting nothing more than to be near Him. They start doing the things they did at first such as studying His Word with others and joining them

---

114. See Heb. 9:27.

for meals, prayer, and conversation. They begin serving others, ordering their time, their money, and their gifts around God's desires for them. In other words, they grow and mature. As they reach a certain place on their journey with God, they have less of a need to be spoon-fed by others and more of a conviction that they should be showing up to help others who are as they were. They start discipling other people (although very few are aware that that is what they are actually doing), saying yes to opportunities to lead short-term mission trips, staying up late with the high schoolers, or spending their weekends leading a Bible study.

At some point, our understanding of doctrine is meant to become a skeleton rather than flesh. It is always present, never seen directly, but the effects of it are as clear as day. That is where our latent neurosis and fear-of-man issues come into play. Depending on the stream of Christianity you swim in, there are certain expectations to ensure your doctrinal credibility by making sure you use the right language to drop hints that you are a well-informed Christian. To not do so is to risk becoming the target of well-meaning teachers who post up at the gates of heaven, ready to correct any wrong belief you may hold. How could Jesus possibly be the center of our life without assuring others that we are "gospel-centered"? Our natural desire is to fit in at all costs, so we unknowingly comply, playing the game to earn our belonging.

In other streams, a narrow understanding of the Bible is revered as the third person of the Trinity, and in order to believe anything, you must proof the text with chapter and verse. There is no gentle invitation to walk beyond the borders with Jesus, just a rigid adherence to the finished product of our English Bibles. Still other streams prize the experience so much that in order to belong, you must downplay the importance of doctrine, manufacturing a real, passionate love for Jesus at all times that never doubts, gets angry, or uses bad words in prayer. As Ed Friedman said in his seminal work, "The acceptance and even cherishing of uncertainty is critical to keeping the human mind from voyaging into the delusion of omniscience."[115]

M. Scott Peck developed what he called the four stages of spiritual development,[116] contributing to a long and full history of others who have done the same. The first stage is chaos and disorder due to an unwillingness to accept a power outside of ourselves. Stage 2 is institutional, where we first come across some belief, knowledge, or idea that helps make sense of that chaos and follow it without question. The third stage is skepticism and deconstruction of things we once took by faith but now need something logical to support. Stage 4 is communion where we finally come to embrace the wonder and mystery of the world around us that evades such neat definitions and explanations. Such a person's spirituality has moved past blind faith and past deconstruction, and lives with genuine belief. We all know people who have gotten to a place in their lives where their growth became stunted either from a blind devotion to the institutional stage or due to their extended deconstruction of things they once believed blindly. Because we feel an almost primal desire to remain safe and protected, we can use doctrine as a cloak to hide us from dealing with such troubling thoughts.

One sermon series I was especially proud of was a look at the psalms of David via the narrative stories in Samuel, Chronicles,

---

115. Edwin H. Friedman, *A Failure of Nerve: Leadership in the Age of the Quick Fix* (New York: Church Publishing, 2017), 52.
116. M. Scott Peck, MD, *The Different Drum: Community Making and Peace* (New York: Touchstone, 1998), 187.

and Kings. The series was called "Songs of David," and every week I took one of the psalms written in direct response to something that happened in David's life and explored the emotions he expressed through song. It was too much for some people who left our church because they believed I was not preaching the gospel. Even though the good news of Jesus shined through every narrative, I was using unfamiliar, uncomfortable language to try to bring new life to familiar songs.

Another time, I did a three-week series on our core values of gospel, community, and mission. The first week (gospel), I was accused of being too heady and theological, leaving out community and global mission. The second week (community), I was accused of being too sentimental and idealistic, not talking about God's purpose for this community. The third week (mission), I was accused of not mentioning the gospel as the impetus that changes people enough to cause them to desire to live missionally. I can't make this stuff up.

If we are to pay attention to God, we must use intellectual assent, doctrinal belief, and familiar language for their intended purpose—an unsafe, unscripted glimpse of God's glory, tearing the fabric of our ordinary lives. It's a reminder of His power and glory, despite our weaknesses and unimpressiveness. It's a kind of experience that our neat sermons don't prepare us for, something that no chart or graph of the end times or eschatology can produce in us. We need to truly and actually believe that the living God speaks today, wants to commune and communicate with us, and desires our attention. It is only this attention that displaces fear, replaces anxiety, and generally makes us spiritually wise and attentive people who stand near God, ready to listen when called upon, ready to speak in and out of season, and quick to encourage others with the good news.

The late philosopher and theologian Dallas Willard regularly insisted this:

> *It is the failure to understand Jesus and his words as reality and vital information about life that explains why, today, we do not routinely teach those who profess allegiance to him how to do what he said was best. More than any other single thing, in any case, the* practical irrelevance of actual obedience *to Christ accounts for the weakened effect of Christianity in the world today, with its increasing tendency to emphasize political and social action as the primary way to serve God. It also accounts for the practical irrelevance of Christian faith to individual character development and overall personal sanity and well-being.*[117]

Once we have paused to reflect and taken the time to pay attention to our inner selves (soul), we are ready to actively engage with God. This time, we do so without pretense, embarrassingly honest yet approaching Him without condemnation or judgment. We are ready to go beyond the borders of safety, which sounds great in song but is much more difficult to breach in life. To actually do such a thing requires risk. It requires taking the risk of being wrong, needing to apologize, and being willing to admit when it was our own pride leading us rather than the Spirit. Little is safe about passionately following Jesus with abandon. There is little to no path already trampled that repels some and draws others. We can't look to others for a step-by-step playbook and must coalesce advice, knowledge of

---

117. Dallas Willard, *The Divine Conspiracy: Rediscovering Our Hidden Life in God* (New York: HarperCollins, 1998), xiv–xv.

Scripture, and a nudge from God to walk boldly. The familiar saying "A ship in harbor is safe—but that is not what ships are built for" describes our gut feeling at this moment.

My conviction is that seasons of extended waiting prepare us for this kind of risk. They actually make us fed up with our current reality so we can hone and clarify our deepest desires and be empowered to set sail for some uncharted course. We are simultaneously as bold as Paul. "If God is for us, who can be against us?" (Rom. 8:31). We are as scared as Abraham who allowed his wife to become part of Pharaoh's harem to avoid being hurt or killed. Unlike our childish fears, the dangers and threats are real, yet we walk with God through them. The thing about bravery is that it feels eerily similar to foolishness in the moment. Every voice of reason, every giant on our shoulder, every naysayer whispering in our ear come alive to give us a multitude of reasons why we are doomed to fail. The only thing we have going for us is the voice of God, and sometimes we doubt that as well.

Still, the prime location for real, adaptive change is where we are out of our comfort zones, in unfamiliar terrain. Think of a short-term mission trip you've taken or some kind of service project where the team was bound together in less-than-ideal circumstances to do something greater than themselves. We intuitively know the mental, physical, and spiritual stretching that comes from some kind of difficulty to be true. In their book about the intersection of the laws of tradition and the forces of transformation called *Surfing the Edge of Chaos*, Pascale, Millemann, and Gioja explain:

> *Nature is at its innovative best near the edge of chaos. . . . The edge of chaos is a condition, not a location. . . . Moving to the edge of chaos creates*

upheaval but not dissolution. That's why being on the edge is so important. The edge is not the abyss. It's the sweet spot for productive change. . . . And when the productive agitation runs high, innovation often thrives and startling breakthroughs can come about.[118]

Being on the frontlines of risk displaces our comfort zones but does so without dysfunction. We are simultaneously safe yet provoked. This is how new experiences with the God-Who-Saves, the God-Who-Sees, and the God-Who-Provides are built. It is only when we put ourselves in situations where our only hope is for God to be who He said He is and do what He said He would do that we can witness the miraculous. These experiences lead us to commit to a course we know is right such as when Hernán Cortés arrived in the New World in 1519 with 600 men and when safely on shore burned his ships. That sent a clear message to his men that there would be no turning back.

When we hedge our bets and play it safe, that is the proportion to which we experience the Holy Spirit. Though He still indwells us, though He still illuminates Scripture, and though He still comforts us, we simply don't need God to do the miraculous. Even if God doesn't show up, we still have it covered. Having been freed from the prison of always being right, never apologizing and never being seen as weak and foolish, we are free to joyfully live without the masks that we used both to hide and keep us safe from others for so long.

---

118. Richard T. Pascale, Mark Millemann, and Linda Gioja, *Surfing the Edge of Chaos: The Laws of Nature and the New Laws of Business* (New York: Crown Publishing Group, 2001), 61.

God becomes less of a figurehead for our daddy issues and more of a parent, tender enough to hold us and strong enough to command the forces of nature and all of human history. Jesus becomes less of an idea to wrestle with and more of a person to adventure with. The Spirit of God becomes less a mental puzzle to decipher and more a felt reality of empowerment and encouragement. It turns out that waiting unlocks new facets of our relationship with God that we never dared believe before. All the hard work, soul searching, and pride humbling were a doorway to a new world of joy, freedom, and hope.

In his conclusion of *The Chronicles of Narnia* series, C. S. Lewis describes the final doorway to Aslan's country as a stable door. Some who saw Aslan for the first time were filled with terror and hatred and wandered off into the darkness, not daring to believe anything so wild could be good. Those who dared to believe Aslan's word walked through the door to find "a deeper country: every rock and flower and blade of grass looked as if it meant more."[119] It was more real than anything they had previously experienced. Yet the doorway to this beautiful world was narrow and uncertain, and required faith to walk through it. What are we missing out on by settling for a version of God that forgives and takes away our sins but doesn't make us into the kind of people we wish we were? Dallas Willard once famously said, "God's intent for us is that we would become the kind of persons that he can empower to do what we want."[120] That's clever, complex, and a little difficult to swallow. Aren't we supposed to be the kind of people who do whatever God wants?

119. C. S. Lewis, *The Last Battle* (New York: HarperCollins, 1956), 213.
120. Bill Gaultiere, "Dallas Willard's Definitions and Quotes," Soulshepherding, accessed June 22, 2021, https://www.soulshepherding.org/dallas-willards-definitions/.

Not if we have become the kind of person for whom there is no difference.

I started this chapter with a quote by John O'Donohue: "You have traveled too fast over false ground / Now your soul has come to take you back."[121] In the same poem, he encourages quietness and courage by saying, "Imitate the habit of twilight / Taking time to open the well of color / that fostered the brightness of day. / Draw alongside the silence of stone / Until its calmness can claim you."[122] I love the imagery of our true self being compared to the hues of twilight. As the sun is setting, we see all the colors that made up the brightest part of the day.

As you read this, I don't know where you are. I know neither your past nor your present reality. I certainly do not know what God will do for you in the future. I do know you are right now receiving some kind of invitation to trust and follow Jesus. Whether you accept it, put it off for another day, or convince yourself it didn't happen is up to you. I ask you to have the courage to believe that something no eye has seen and no ear has heard is being prepared for you. It's something that will propel you to vulnerably walk in the light where safety is not guaranteed. You will dare to swim out of the shallows where it gets dark and you can't touch the bottom, but it is more real than anything you've ever experienced. Press forward knowing God is smiling just as big as you are while you discover more of yourself and Him in the process.

---

121. Excerpt from "For One Who Is Exhausted," and Excerpt from "For the Interim Time" from TO BLESS THE SPACE BETWEEN US A BOOK OF BLESSINGS by John O'Donohue, copyright © 2008 by John O'Donohue. Used by permission of Doubleday, an imprint of the Knopf Doubleday Publishing Group, a division of Penguin Random House LLC. All rights reserved.
122. Ibid.

Φ

CHAPTER NINE:
FOLLOWING JESUS
THROUGH DIFFERENT
SEASONS OF LIFE

Experience bereaves us of our innocence. Wisdom
bereaves us of our ignorance.

—Henry David Thoreau

Some years ago, I was in rural Iowa doing some training for cross-cultural global workers when I had a cross-cultural experience myself. I asked my hosts if they would take me to some real Iowa farms. Being a city boy with soft hands, I had never lived or spent much time in the Midwest and certainly not around farms. They chuckled a little at my request but were good sports about it and drove me to visit a couple farms.

While visiting one of the farms, I talked to an older man who had been a farmer his whole life. He recounted the last several years of crops and mentioned that the previous winter had

been particularly brutal. With something of a distant look, he
remarked, "That's the thing about bad years. The only thing you
can do is wait for the ground to thaw and begin another season
of planting." His comfort was knowing that one year's harvest (or
lack of) will be followed by another opportunity. Until we die or
Jesus returns, no season of our lives has the final word. Winter
is designed to be the womb that sustains life until it gives way to
spring. The enjoyment of summer gives way to autumn's harvest,
and then the cycle begins again. Sometimes one season starts
early, lasts long, or skips the next, but change it must.

It is with good reason Jesus compares our life in Him to a
branch and a vine. Here's what Jesus teaches us:

> *I am the true vine, and my Father is the vinedresser.
> Every branch in me that does not bear fruit he takes
> away, and every branch that does bear fruit he
> prunes, that it may bear more fruit. Already you are
> clean because of the word that I have spoken to you.
> Abide in me, and I in you. As the branch cannot bear
> fruit by itself, unless it abides in the vine, neither can
> you, unless you abide in me. I am the vine; you are
> the branches. Whoever abides in me and I in him,
> he it is that bears much fruit, for apart from me you
> can do nothing. If anyone does not abide in me he
> is thrown away like a branch and withers; and the
> branches are gathered, thrown into the fire, and
> burned. If you abide in me, and my words abide in
> you, ask whatever you wish, and it will be done for
> you. By this my Father is glorified, that you bear
> much fruit and so prove to be my disciples.*
>
> —John 15:1–8

We are told to abide, or dwell, in Jesus and allow His Word to abide, or live, in us. The illustration of a vineyard is apropos. There are several seasons in the life of a branch on the vine, from springtime budding to winter dormancy. As Jesus taught, there are different needs and requirements to keep the vine healthy during different seasons. Maintenance of a vine in the winter requires pruning branches and in the summer requires a process known as "suckering," or thinning and trimming excess shoots for greater fruitfulness in the fall. How do we follow Jesus in the different seasons of our lives? How can we move from pining for a life that always reflects summer to the actual lives we live full of pruning, ripening, and blooming?

Winter

The stillness of a vineyard during dormancy can lead us to believe that nothing is happening, but we would be mistaken. Dormancy may be a stagnant state, but this state preserves life. Winter comes right after the late autumn pruning as the leaves start to fall, giving the land the impression of going from dying to death. Instead, life is actually being preserved during cold, inhospitable months, even as it appears to be dead. In the vineyard, that is the time to prepare the fields for the coming year, repair equipment, get ready, and settle debts for the present year.

It's interesting that we understand winter dormancy to be a natural occurrence in the physical world, but we somehow never expect it in the spiritual realm. We are taken off guard when our lives are on anything other than an upward trajectory, filled with success, winning, growing finances, and joy. We foolishly expect an eternal summer in our lives, and we view any hint of winter with suspicion, dread, or disbelief. We can call the very things that make for our greatest growth either curses or punishment from God. How interesting for a faith that worships a God who became man in order to take on the suffering of humanity to not know what to do with their own suffering when it happens to them.

During Holy Week, the week leading up to the death and resurrection of Jesus, there is a time on the church calendar known as *Sabbatum Sanctum,* Latin for Holy Sabbath. Sometimes called Holy Saturday or the Great Sabbath, it marks the day after the death of Jesus when His physical body lay in the tomb while His Spirit descended into Hades in order to bring salvation to the righteous dead. The Apostle Paul speaks of this event in Ephesians 4:10: "He who descended is the one who also ascended far above all the heavens, that he might fill all things."

There is so much meaning and purpose in this little recognized day that it deserves time and space to meditate on the dormant space between Good Friday and Resurrection Sunday. While the death and resurrection of Jesus have become popular cultural observances, it is worth noting that a period of dormancy is needed in order for life to come from death. Holy Saturday reminds us that while the physical body of Jesus lay lifeless in a tomb, seemingly abandoned by God and defeated, His Spirit was accomplishing salvation for every saint who ever has died or will die. Jesus became the firstfruit of the dead so we, whose bodies will surely return to dust, will also live again with Him. The famous woodcarving by Albrecht Durer, the *Harrowing of Hell,* is called "Christ's Descent into Limbo." It shows a half-clothed Jesus reaching underground to pull a man up out of a hole while the saints watch, holding a banner and a cross. At the same time, a demon emerges from another pit on top with a spear pointed at Jesus. Both the great cloud of witnesses[123] and the hordes of hell are watching as Jesus fulfills what He died to do.

---

123. See Heb. 12:1.

Dormancy in the winter of our soul also feels like harrowing when we are confined to waiting. We too are in between heaven and hell, waiting for the work that Jesus began to be completed in us. *Harrowing* is an interesting word. As an adjective, it refers to something incredibly distressing. As a noun, it refers to an agricultural instrument with sharp teeth dragged over plowed land in order to break up clods of dirt or remove weeds. That is a good picture of how it feels during the quiet of Holy Saturday. There has already been some kind of death, loss, grief, and pain, yet new life has not sprung from the ashes quite yet. Instead, Jesus is at work harrowing our hearts, breaking up clots of hardened plaque, removing the weeds of doubt, of idolatry, of selfishness. Anything that keeps us from truly experiencing resurrection life is an invitation for Jesus to ruthlessly destroy it. Though we may lose the thing that seems to be the very source of our joy and life, if it is something that has replaced Jesus as the object of our affections, we can rest knowing it is for our good that it is removed.

It is a harrowing experience to feel completely laid bare and open, yet it is strangely comforting knowing that the One holding the harrow has also been completely laid bare and open. The great joy of the gospel is that we follow a Savior not just in word or command but in example. It pleased the Father to allow Jesus to experience all that makes us truly human, including suffering, that He might learn obedience through the things He suffered.[124] If our Master was a man of sorrows, acquainted with grief, who learned obedience through suffering, and if a servant is not greater than his master,[125] then it stands to reason that we, too, will walk that plowed road at one time or another. Because there is no longer any

---

124. See Heb. 5:8.
125. See Matt. 10:24.

fear in love,[126] we can walk toward desolation, knowing there is not a drop of punishment left. It is an invitation from a loving Savior who longs to heal us from our wounds, even those that have been self-inflicted. This invitation requires only our acquiescence to the process. It is harrowing in every sense of the word, yet there is a reason behind it. God is making us more like Jesus with the capacity to love more deeply than we thought possible by hurting more acutely than we ever wished. The two go hand in hand since each is required in order for the other to thrive.

And in order for us to love with all our heart, mind, soul, and strength, sometimes it is necessary for us to lose each of those for a season to reinforce that Jesus actually wants to be our strength in weakness and wisdom in our foolishness.[127] And so we wait in the tomb, feeling lifeless and dead in our bodies, while the Spirit of God is working healing and restoration to our souls. We learn to value the spiritual, which cannot be taken away more than the physical that we cannot hold on to forever. We develop the eyes of faith, able to see the possibility of a new hope and future even while in the depths of the earth. The pain of death and waiting becomes our invitation to follow Jesus into the dark, trusting without answers and waiting without evidence.

Spring

As Henry David Thoreau observed, "We discover a new world every time that we see the earth again after it has been covered for a season with snow."[128] I don't know if it's the newness of the season or our renewed eyesight that causes this, but I'm always amazed

---

126. See 1 John 4:18.
127. See 1 Cor. 1:25.
128. Henry David Thoreau, *The Writings of Henry David Thoreau, Volume 19* (London: Wentworth Press, 2016).

by how new spring feels. Winter dormancy inevitably gives way to spring budding when seasonal growth resumes. Budding is the very first sign of life on the vine, and though it's still far from harvest fruit, the budding is a promise of what is to come. This period is marked by hopefulness and joy after a long winter, and at this stage, the ultimate success of the year's crop depends on the maintenance of the vineyard. That is what Jesus refers to as pruning. Every branch that is actually alive and bearing fruit needs to be pruned in order to bear more fruit. The vinedresser has to clean out what is left over from winter's dying plants, gather seeds, decide which fields to plow, ensure sufficient resources, and sow the land during the season.

Following Jesus during the springtime of our lives doesn't require perseverance or determination since the air itself is ripe with possibility. Hope flows from every action, thought, and desire, though all of life's dreams are not yet materialized. But just as the quality of the crop depends on the maintenance, so the seeds planted in the spring will grow for good or bad. Budding is the very first sign of life on the vines in spring when the vines enter a rapid growing period when leaves and buds shoot out from the vines and start to form the clusters that will ultimately become grapes.

So it is in our lives. The seasons of spring in our soul bring life, activity, and the promise of fruit. Yet as Robert Louis Stevenson once said, "Don't judge each day by the harvest you reap but by the seeds that you plant."[129]

After a particularly long winter of my soul, I was waiting for spring to come. I had gone through several hard years of harrowing,

---

129. Robert Louis Stevenson, *Admiral Guinea* (Exton: A Word to the Wise Publishing, 2013).

plowing up the hard soil of my soul, and I was more than ready for it to be over. While I was expecting a word from the Lord to tell me it was time to pick up my mat and move on, my spring came in an unexpected way. After a long season of rest, reevaluation, and repentance, Jesus led my family to begin the journey of welcoming neglected children from the foster care system into our home. Our first placement, the one with four siblings ages 1, 2, 4, and 7, happened during the first week of the state-mandated quarantine due to COVID-19. We eagerly welcomed the children at about 1:30 in the morning. They had just been removed from their mother's home. All our lives were turned upside down in this season, so we just rolled with the stress, difficulty, and emotions that came with this time.

Later, we finally had the opportunity to take the kids for a physical visit with their mother, and I realized this was an experience that was brand-new to me. Never have I found myself in this situation or anything like it that would have prepared me for the awkwardness of meeting a mother deemed unfit by the state yet deeply loved and missed by her children. Never have I experienced the gut-wrenching feeling of taking a young child from the arms of her mother and returning to our home while she returned to hers to deal with a drug problem. It was on that day that the weight of the work Jesus was doing in the long, slow quiet of the previous years buoyed our souls in the present moment. I turned to my wife and said, "I think it's done." The winter of our souls had passed, and we found new strength, new hope, and new energy in this new endeavor. Up until that point, I had not felt healed, nor had I known that spring would come without fanfare.

Sometimes God uses circumstances to move us from one season to the next, even without our knowing it. I relished the feeling of being allowed to undertake such a worthy task, equally knowing how unfit and unprepared I was for it. Spring came, not from my own efforts or preparation but from the grace of the Father who calls us into the kind of work that requires His attention and presence in order to remain faithful. I was aware that Jesus would use this time to shape our lives forever, but I was freed from the need to control the outcome. It was new for me, someone who was used to grasping tightly to my ideas and plans, to relinquish control in the trust of One who led me and my family to this place of service. I thought of Gandalf's words to King Théoden in *The Lord of the Rings*: "Your fingers would remember their old strength better, if they grasped a sword-hilt."[130] I felt the familiar strength of the Lord while I reengaged with the work of serving others, albeit from a different posture. Like Théoden, I felt I was waking up from a long sleep to engage with the world around me as a free man.

In the springtime seasons of our lives, new life breathes into familiar rhythms. Like the first day it is warm enough to put something on the grill and enjoy a meal outside, this time is familiar but still feels really good. What lay dormant in winter reemerges with new fervor. While spring will give way to late summer when we once again long to wear sweatshirts in front of a fire, for now we can simply enjoy the newness of life all around us—flowers blooming, beaches filling up with people, and longer days. It is at this time that possibilities delayed by winter come to fruition and our joy is full. It is also at this time when we need to recommit to walking with Jesus, not just working for Him. The danger is that we can adopt a self-sufficient posture, enjoying the gifts God has showered without enjoying the Giver Himself.

---

130. J. R. R. Tolkien, *The Two Towers* (Boston, MA: Houghton Mifflin Company, 1954), 121.

Many of us know the feeling of accomplishing a task we have been uniquely called to do. It is an incredibly empowering feeling when "the place God calls you to is the place where your deep gladness and the world's deep hunger meet."[131] It is also here where we can feel sufficient within ourselves and forget that Jesus is the One who created this joy for Him to sustain. We were created for a life with God, from God. Ultimately, our enjoyment of this season is tied to our enjoyment of Jesus, the bringer of spring. Even in the experience of new life cropping up everywhere, there is the familiar ache of winter, reminding us that the same Jesus who walks with us in victory is the very same One who encourages us to trust Him when there is no fruit to be seen. Regardless how long or how intense this season is, Jesus is the same yesterday, today, and forever.[132] So we walk forward in confidence and joy, knowing that even the residual limp is a gift from God.

Summer

In summer, the vineyard's fruit is now growing and ripening. Weather (outside our control) now dictates the quality of the crop, while maintenance continues to aid development. Summer is about tending to what has taken root and allowing the fruit to ripen to perfection. There is no pruning during this season, but caretakers still thin and trim leaves. They need to protect the plants from insects or disease. They need to water, fertilize, and continue to monitor and prune the crops.

---

131. Frederick Buechner, *Wishful Thinking: A Seeker's ABC* (San Francisco: HarperOne, 1993).
132. See Heb. 13:8.

Parker Palmer says:

Summer is the season when all the promissory notes of autumn and winter and spring come due, and each year the debts are repaid with compound interest. In summer, it is hard to remember that we had ever doubted the natural process, had ever ceded death the last word, had ever lost faith in the powers of new life. Summer is a reminder that our faith is not nearly as strong as the things we profess to have faith in—a reminder that, for this single season at least, we might cease our anxious machinations and give ourselves to the abiding and abundant grace of our common life.[133]

In summer, it is hard to remember we ever doubted the natural process, and that is the point. It is a gift from God that our souls are so bombarded with goodness that we forget the chill of winter for a while. It is a time for healing and enjoyment, for playing and laughing, and for appreciating "the abiding and abundant grace of our common life."[134]

Yet instead of enjoying this abundance, sometimes we feel guilty for it, making excuses and telling ourselves it's not okay for us to enjoy this season when so many others cannot. We think of people experiencing their own winter season and feel we have no right to enjoy a summer of our own. Not only is this unwise but there is no spiritual advantage in choosing not to enjoy God's abundant goodness during this season. In fact, our reasons for

---

133. Parker Palmer, *Seasons: A Center for Renewal*, The Fetzer Institute, 26, https://fetzer.org/sites/default/files/images/stories/pdf/seasonsbook.pdf.
134. Ibid.

avoiding enjoyment may uncover underlying fears. We may be afraid to enjoy something only to have God take it away. We may be afraid that the glimpse of good will awaken the familiar ache of it coming to an end. We may struggle with guilt and fear of being thought of as a bad friend. We all know that the party will come to an end, but that shouldn't keep us from enjoying what we can while we can. The knowledge that this season must come to an end is the only invitation we need to enjoy it while it lasts.

Aesop once said it is possible to have too much of a good thing, and that is true in summer. We are hardy creatures of the earth, invigorated by challenge and effort. We were not made to waste away in Margaritaville, and though that sounds great at times, deep down we know we would just get bored and crave something new. When spring gives way to summer, I am the first to trade jeans for shorts, fire up the grill every night, and spend as much time in the water as I can, paddle boarding and swimming. School lets out, and our family adopts a completely different rhythm of life than we do any other time of the year. Yet toward the end of the season, in what we call the dog days of summer, I miss blankets, fires on a rainy day, and my favorite hoodie. Even the kids, who just two months ago were counting down the last days of school, start to miss their friends, their school environment, and their normal routines. Because we know this season happens every year and that it is good and right for it to happen, we need not fear drinking deeply of the abundance of summer. It is a respite in our year to enjoy all God has been doing, take family vacations, and spend an inordinate amount of time playing together. Fall is coming, and with it there will be another round of good work to be done. By letting the soil of our lives lie fallow for a season, we can enter autumn ready for whatever God calls us.

Autumn

We are tempted to view harvest season as the main event every year, as if each subsequent season exists to serve the coming harvest. To some degree, it is the season with the most movement and inherent urgency. Vinedressers must get the crops out of the field before they rot or are damaged by the elements. The harvesting must be done quickly and efficiently. It is also the season where the labor of spring and summer pays off as we get to enjoy what took so long to grow.

But to view autumn as the well-earned weekend to a mundane work week would be shortsighted. More enjoyment on the surface does not automatically translate to being better, truer, or more significant. That kind of thinking is like falling in the trap of believing that God is with us only if enjoyment and ease accompany Him. We also feel some sadness during harvest since each season contains either the seeds or fruit of each other. When we see a season appear that took forever to arrive, we remember the tears, the darkness, the toil, and the desires that led us to this place. We remember the shouting matches with God, the incessant doubt, the pessimism and fatalism as our hearts were blinded by what our eyes could not see. And we resolve that by next autumn, we won't fall into the same trap again. We will remember that God's Word never returns void, that His promises never fail, and that His love will always drown out our fears if we let it. In some way, we are encouraged each year as well. From faith to faith and glory to glory, we see some measure of small change and slight growth, enough to lead us to continue to plant new seeds and trust the process. It is enough to remind us during the cold winter months that life is just under the surface covered with snow.

Harvesting the fruit of our labors is meant to be savored and enjoyed, tempered all the more by the fact that we have submitted to the course of each prior season. Whether we find ourselves in the dormancy of winter or the pregnant sunrise of spring, we have labored to remain present, aware, and ever watchful, doing the needed interior work that allows us to make better sense of the external changes all around us. For this reason, pure, unadulterated enjoyment is *required* in the fall. We have given ourselves to be present in every other season, and for us to remain present and aware during autumn's harvest requires a deep enjoyment of the goodness and bounty of God. We need not continue with a scarcity mentality when God desires us to drink deeply from His well that satisfies. That satisfaction may very well come from an exceptional year of grapes that produce the wine that brings joy. It may come from a particularly tasty crop of fresh fruits and vegetables to harvest and eat by themselves or alongside another feast. Likewise, that satisfaction may come from a difficulty weathered, a relational conflict turned learning experience, or some painful revisiting of the past that will pave the way for a healthier future.

On this side of fall, some of us can't enjoy these sweet times without preemptively qualifying them. We have not yet been trained by grace enough to recognize that provision and contentment are fall's close cousins with more than a hint of similarity. Instead of stuffing our faces full of the goodness in front of us, we rehearse why we are not worthy to enjoy such goodness. We remember all our foibles, flaws, frailty, and faults. Our blemishes and inadequacies seem too concrete and demand some kind of appeasement. If this description sounds like you, remember that the gospel is called the good news primarily for this reason. Against all hope and beyond our wildest dreams, we are told that God sees, knows, and accepts every part of us. We are also told that Jesus came to rescue us by taking off the old, shameful rags that were a potent reminder of a lifetime of failure.

Not only does He take them from us, He puts them on Himself and stands in our place between the judgment of heaven and the condemnation of hell. Having absorbed our rebellion against God and satisfied the wrath of God against our sin, He dresses us again, this time with clean, pure robes of righteousness. From this point on, when God views us, He sees us through the finished work of Jesus Christ, which leaves us not just forgiven of sin but also without the stain of guilt that accompanies it.[135]

What Christ accomplished on the cross for His redeemed was, is, and forever will be total and complete. There is no measure of condemnation left to remind us of our past failures. There is not the smallest trace of exasperation from a God wondering when we are going to finally get our act together and start living up to our potential. There is only the gaze of love, pleasure, and delight in us, not in a future iteration of us but the *us* that we have such a hard time loving right now. God knows Christ's sacrifice was sufficient to cover the remaining imperfections and blemishes and that it will also take a lifetime to see Him work them out. It is not for nothing that the Old Testament constantly reminds us that God is patient,[136] loving, slow to anger, and quick to forgive. Yet we continue to labor under an imagined harsh taskmaster who sounds more like an earthly father who was never pleased with us, a harsh, distant judge, or a rule-giver waiting for us to slip up so he can say "I told you so." Some forms of self-loathing run so deep that we need the Bible to affirm God's delight in us again and again, both as His creation and as His children. Because this is the best news in the world, we can fill our glasses to overflowing and drink long to satisfy the insatiable.

---

135. See 1 John 1:9, Isa. 61:10, Eph. 4:24.
136. See 2 Pet. 3:9, 3:15; Ps. 103:8; Exod. 34:6; Num. 14:18.

No matter the season, there will always be a fresh invitation to follow Jesus. It might be to steel ourselves against the chill of winter as we prepare to be more dormant than we would like. It may be a season of spring cleaning, purging some old habits and well-trodden paths of distraction to make room for newer, life-giving habits. Maybe it is the invitation to enjoy our Creator and Sustainer whose goodness and mercy follow us for His name's sake, not because of our hard work.

You might be in a busy harvest season, reaping seeds previously sown by the sweat of your brow. In work and in rest, it is always the right season to ask two questions: Where is Jesus at work in my life? What is Jesus doing through this season? The answers are sure to yield their own kind of harvest in your life.

BU
TTERF
LY

Shimmer of light, flashes of color
Disorienting sounds, clear and loud
Brightness from within and without
A moment of pause, trying to remember what once was.
The first thing I feel is the lightness
The weight and the hunger have changed
The next thing I hear are the voices
In hushed silence, no longer telling me who I am
But watching with awe and wonder
Waiting for me to announce my new name
Though no longer heavy and hungry
I reach for what I know
To crawl and to chew, to consume what I need
Not recognizing that is gone as well
These wet appendages, now dry in the sun
Flutter open in the warmth of the day
Revealing not legs, but glorious wings
And elicit more praise from the voices
A Monarch! A Queen! A Ruler! they say
As they look on my bright colored wings
And now for the first time, I look
Without even trying, it seems
The best part is the hunger, or lack of, I notice
No longer do I yearn for the leaf of the earth,
but the nectar of flower.

A food fitting for the Queen I am.
Through nothing I have done, it seems I now have
A tongue perfectly shaped to drink it
Is this some cosmic joke, or a beautiful story
Both, it now seems to me
No longer needing to be loved, but finding I am
I fly, for the first time, quite free
Without limits nor restraint, I no longer need
Small fingers to walk on for value
Yet should I choose to brighten their day

I may land on a shoulder or hand
You are special (so I tell them), you too can be free
Though toil and tears are part of the plan
Now the main part of life I remember
Can be summed up in just two things:
The larva I was
The butterfly I am
But little of the crucible between.

EPILOGUE:
GOING OUT WEEPING,
COMING HOME SINGING

When the LORD restored the fortunes of Zion,
we were like those who dream.
Then our mouth was filled with laughter,
and our tongue with shouts of joy;
then they said among the nations,
"The LORD has done great things for them."
The LORD has done great things for us;
we are glad.

Restore our fortunes, O LORD,
like streams in the Negeb!
Those who sow in tears
shall reap with shouts of joy!
He who goes out weeping,
bearing the seed for sowing,
shall come home with shouts of joy,
bringing his sheaves with him.

—Ps. 126

This psalm was written after God released the Jewish exiles from their captivity and restored them to Jerusalem after 70 years. Their joy and excitement are described as feeling like a dream. Like those who can't believe their own eyes, they surveyed their homeland for the first time in almost an entire generation, and it seemed too good to be true. After years of being displaced in a country and culture so different from their own, they were finally home. Extended periods of liminality often feel like a journey to a far country. We emerge feeling like foreigners to our own life, estranged from familiar routines, work, relationships, or other rhythms we are used to. We know we are meant to praise God in the storm and walk with Him through it, but we also know that it is easier in concept than practice. If we were previously addicted to a pace of life that did not allow God to meet us in deafening silence, the feeling of forward movement again can be a rush. It truly can feel like a spirit of heaviness has been replaced by garments of praise.[137]

Either way, the experience of joy, so full that our mouths are filled with laughter and singing, is something to behold. As the Jewish nation celebrated being brought home after a long captivity, we celebrate during periods of transitioning out of liminal spaces. When the season of feeling stuck between something we had to let go of and something we are reaching for is distinctly over, it is appropriate to allow the completeness of the joy to wash over us. It doesn't mean we are done waiting for the Lord as a practice and a habit, but a season of our lives marked by waiting is finally over, and that feels great. Yet even when reaping the fruit of our tears, there are still tears left. Some are tears of joy; others are tears of regret or pain. We always carry some wounds with us, and they end up becoming integrated with all the other experiences that make us who we are. As the poet Rumi said, "The wound is the place where the Light enters you."[138]

137. See Isa. 61:3.
138. "Rumi Quotes," Goodreads, accessed June 22, 2021, https://www.good reads.com/quotes/1299504-i-said-what-about-my-eyes-he-said-keep-them.

Even while celebrating, the psalmist recognizes that the work of restoration has just begun and asks God to send a river of favor and blessing in the dry, arid land of Negeb. A tension grows there as the work behind us and the work ahead begin to coexist in the same life. Brokenness and beauty live in the same house, always. Tangible victories are behind us, yet we still wait on the finished work of the cross to have its way in our life. This tension is what allows those who sow in tears to reap in joy. Long periods of hard work and waiting give way to tears of joy. We want to reap the joy without sowing the tears, but we know that is not the way life works. God knows us so well that if He were to give the experience of joy without the waiting and work, it would not be fulfilling or meaningful to us. Without the long hours of work and anticipation, we would have no reason to treasure something long waited for. It's interesting to note the contrast between the immediacy of a desert like the Negeb being suddenly filled by a river in verse 4 and the long planting, sowing, and reaping process that comes only after a long period of hard work and waiting.

I have an unpopular opinion when it comes to liminality, time, and healing. It has been said that the only thing that will bring healing from pain and suffering is time—"Time heals all wounds," as the saying goes. I agree with author Anne Morrow Lindbergh (wife of famed aviator Charles Lindbergh), who said, "I do not believe that sheer suffering teaches. If suffering alone taught, all the world would be wise, since everyone suffers. To suffering must be added mourning, understanding, patience, love, openness and the willingness to remain vulnerable."[139]

Since suffering is common to all yet clearly does not produce the same outcome in every individual, it requires more than time

---

139. Anne Morrow Lindbergh, *Gift from the Sea* (New York: Pantheon, 1991).

for it to have its perfect work in us. I am always struck by our different responses to pain and suffering in our lives. For one person, suffering makes them stronger, more compassionate, and empathetic. For another, it leaves them bitter, left to spew that bitterness over all who interact with them. I recall one particularly ornery older man in a previous church who was referred to by another elderly gentleman in the church as "too cantankerous even for us old folks." This ornery man had the gift of time but none of the work it was supposed to do. That is too common to be a fluke.

I resonate deeply with the lyrics of the song "Eight" by Sleeping at Last: "You were wrong, you were wrong, you were wrong—my healing needed more than time."[140] Time alone does not heal, just as time alone does not lead to shouts of joy, bringing loaded sheaves of grain.[141] Our suffering must be processed by spiritual patience and strength coupled with emotional availability and vulnerability. It is precisely during seasons of waiting when we are given the gift of space that can bring all these things together, resulting in a stronger faith, a deeper trust in God, and greater enjoyment of our relationships. And that is one of the greatest gifts that God who abounds in goodness can give.

To those who feel that your best years remain barren while others around you flourish, remember that the first patriarchs did not receive their true names until they were 99 and 90 years old, and they went on to become the father and mother of multitudes. To those of you currently exiled in a wilderness, remember that the desert is where God formed His people's identity. To those

---

140. "Eight," Written by Ryan O'Neal. ©2019 Wine and Song Music (BMI) on behalf of itself & Asteroid B-612. International Copyright Secured All Rights Reserved. Used By Permission
141. See Ps. 126:6.

of you who feel unseen, unappreciated, and unwanted, remember the prophets—of whom the world was not worthy—wandered about in caves and dens. To those of you who feel like Peter after denying Jesus three times—ashamed of your own darkness and unworthy of forgiveness—remember that Jesus did not build His church on the rock until after Peter saw what he was capable of.

We are in good company with the marginalized and the disenfranchised, the disconsolate and the despondent. On the days we are far from doing all things through Christ who strengthens us, He offers love and acceptance. There is one event in the Gospel narratives that has stayed with me for a long time. After climbing to the top of the ladder of Jewish success, believing he had kept every commandment since his youth and still feeling empty, the rich young man in the Bible found that his ladder was leaning against the wrong building. He was so sure to impress Jesus with his credentials that he was unprepared for the seemingly impossible counsel to sell all he had and give it to the poor. Yet before that difficult word from Jesus, there is a brief pause where the text tells us that Jesus looked at him and loved him.[142] There is such encouragement in that brief statement.

I imagine that Jesus is looking at us when we are fingering the fringes of our prayer shawls and phylacteries, proud of our good works and dedication. Instead of calling attention to what we have done, He looks at us, truly looking in our eyes, and recognizes us and loves us. This is not the kind of love that comes from pride in accomplishment but the love of a first-time father watching his infant sleep. I like to prayerfully imagine that scene during my quiet time with Jesus looking at me and loving me. If you feel that practicing some of the things mentioned in this book are too

---

142. See Mark 10:17–22.

difficult for you, just remember that you are loved. It is from that place of being completely loved and perfectly accepted that we can venture into the interior castles of our souls.

It does seem that the longest journey is the journey inward, but the good news is that we have the rest of our lives to explore, being held and kept in perfect peace by the Lover of our souls. May you have the courage to embark on the journey unique to you and find the strength to own your weaknesses and the wisdom to discern God's fingerprints, even in desolate landscapes.

ABOUT THE AUTHOR

Mike Brown lives and works in Los Angeles with Amy, his wife of twenty years, and their four children: Michael, Luke, Hudson, and Grace. A pastor, pioneer, and missiologist, Mike transitioned out of a lead pastor role to start the Family Table, a nonprofit working with vulnerable children and families in the foster care system. If he isn't with his family exploring national parks, you can find him on his paddle board in the Pacific Ocean.

Mike is a writer and speaker who encourages families and equips churches in their foster care and adoption journeys. He also provides consulting for church and organizational leadership teams on strategic planning and effective engagement practices in the foster care/adoption, cross-cultural engagement and justice/community development spheres. For many years, Mike taught strategic church planting and global engagement at Bible colleges, conferences, and through the Perspectives of the World Christian movement across the US and Mexico.

While living in Mexico, Mike and Amy hosted and trained short-term American teams and empowered the local Mexican church. As a pastor, coach, and consultant in an urban city center, he mobilizes gospel communities on mission to the marginalized and underserved. As a foster parent and child welfare advocate, he knows the pain, uncertainty, and loss of loving people in less than ideal circumstances.

Most of his time right now is spent as a foster care advocate as well as coaching church leadership teams to develop and implement strategic and sustainable foster care ministry within their church.

From more than two decades of ministry, Mike has learned how to follow Jesus by learning from the past, living in the present, and embracing an uncertain future held by a steadfast savior.

For more information about the Family Table and how you can practically care for widows and orphans in our midst, visit www.familytable.la or Instagram and Facebook @familytable.la.

To connect with Mike about coaching/consulting requests and all things foster care related, email mike@familytable.la.